C-163

CAREER EXAMINATION SERIES

T0303479

THIS IS YOUR **PASSBOOK**® FOR ...

CONDUCTOR

NLC®
NATIONAL LEARNING CORPORATION®
passbooks.com

NLC®

National Learning Corporation

212 Michael Drive, Syosset, NY 11791
(516) 921-8888 • www.passbooks.com
E-mail: info@passbooks.com

PUBLISHED IN THE UNITED STATES OF AMERICA

PASSBOOK® SERIES

THE *PASSBOOK® SERIES* has been created to prepare applicants and candidates for the ultimate academic battlefield – the examination room.

At some time in our lives, each and every one of us may be required to take an examination – for validation, matriculation, admission, qualification, registration, certification, or licensure.

Based on the assumption that every applicant or candidate has met the basic formal educational standards, has taken the required number of courses, and read the necessary texts, the *PASSBOOK® SERIES* furnishes the one special preparation which may assure passing with confidence, instead of failing with insecurity. Examination questions – together with answers – are furnished as the basic vehicle for study so that the mysteries of the examination and its compounding difficulties may be eliminated or diminished by a sure method.

This book is meant to help you pass your examination provided that you qualify and are serious in your objective.

The entire field is reviewed through the huge store of content information which is succinctly presented through a provocative and challenging approach – the question-and-answer method.

A climate of success is established by furnishing the correct answers at the end of each test.

You soon learn to recognize types of questions, forms of questions, and patterns of questioning. You may even begin to anticipate expected outcomes.

You perceive that many questions are repeated or adapted so that you can gain acute insights, which may enable you to score many sure points.

You learn how to confront new questions, or types of questions, and to attack them confidently and work out the correct answers.

You note objectives and emphases, and recognize pitfalls and dangers, so that you may make positive educational adjustments.

Moreover, you are kept fully informed in relation to new concepts, methods, practices, and directions in the field.

You discover that you arre actually taking the examination all the time: you are preparing for the examination by "taking" an examination, not by reading extraneous and/or supererogatory textbooks.

In short, this PASSBOOK®, used directedly, should be an important factor in helping you to pass your test.

CONDUCTOR

DUTIES

Conductors, under supervision, are responsible for the safe, timely and proper operation of trains. As a Conductor in customer service, opens and closes doors, makes proper announcements to customers and sets up the automatic announcement system, interacts with the Train Operator, Supervision and Control Center when necessary. When performing flagging duties, sets up flags and light signals and takes other required measures for the protection of contractors performing work on or near train ways. As a Platform Conductor, patrols platforms, assists customers in safely entering and exiting trains and assists in the timely dispatch of trains from key stations. When performing yard work, may operate hand-throw switches. Makes reports of unusual occurrences, and performs related work.

EXAMPLES OF TYPICAL TASKS

Walking along subway tracks; stepping over rails (including live third rails); ascending and descending from trains and catwalks to roadbeds; responding to audible signals such as alarm bells, train whistles, horns and radio conversations; responding to visual signals including distinguishing colored lights; using manual equipment related to train operation; remaining in a standing position for extended periods of time; and lifting heavy equipment.

THE TEST:

The multiple-choice test may include questions on understanding and applying written and verbal instructions relative to the safe and efficient duties of a Conductor; using good judgment and taking proper action in emergencies or stressful situations; relating courteously and informatively to the public; the locations of major points of interest; written comprehension, written expression; problem sensitivity; deductive reasoning; inductive reasoning; information ordering; and spatial orientation.

HOW TO TAKE A TEST

I. YOU MUST PASS AN EXAMINATION

A. WHAT EVERY CANDIDATE SHOULD KNOW

Examination applicants often ask us for help in preparing for the written test. What can I study in advance? What kinds of questions will be asked? How will the test be given? How will the papers be graded?

As an applicant for a civil service examination, you may be wondering about some of these things. Our purpose here is to suggest effective methods of advance study and to describe civil service examinations.

Your chances for success on this examination can be increased if you know how to prepare. Those "pre-examination jitters" can be reduced if you know what to expect. You can even experience an adventure in good citizenship if you know why civil service exams are given.

B. WHY ARE CIVIL SERVICE EXAMINATIONS GIVEN?

Civil service examinations are important to you in two ways. As a citizen, you want public jobs filled by employees who know how to do their work. As a job seeker, you want a fair chance to compete for that job on an equal footing with other candidates. The best-known means of accomplishing this two-fold goal is the competitive examination.

Exams are widely publicized throughout the nation. They may be administered for jobs in federal, state, city, municipal, town or village governments or agencies.

Any citizen may apply, with some limitations, such as the age or residence of applicants. Your experience and education may be reviewed to see whether you meet the requirements for the particular examination. When these requirements exist, they are reasonable and applied consistently to all applicants. Thus, a competitive examination may cause you some uneasiness now, but it is your privilege and safeguard.

C. HOW ARE CIVIL SERVICE EXAMS DEVELOPED?

Examinations are carefully written by trained technicians who are specialists in the field known as "psychological measurement," in consultation with recognized authorities in the field of work that the test will cover. These experts recommend the subject matter areas or skills to be tested; only those knowledges or skills important to your success on the job are included. The most reliable books and source materials available are used as references. Together, the experts and technicians judge the difficulty level of the questions.

Test technicians know how to phrase questions so that the problem is clearly stated. Their ethics do not permit "trick" or "catch" questions. Questions may have been tried out on sample groups, or subjected to statistical analysis, to determine their usefulness.

Written tests are often used in combination with performance tests, ratings of training and experience, and oral interviews. All of these measures combine to form the best-known means of finding the right person for the right job.

II. HOW TO PASS THE WRITTEN TEST

A. NATURE OF THE EXAMINATION

To prepare intelligently for civil service examinations, you should know how they differ from school examinations you have taken. In school you were assigned certain definite pages to read or subjects to cover. The examination questions were quite detailed and usually emphasized memory. Civil service exams, on the other hand, try to discover your present ability to perform the duties of a position, plus your potentiality to learn these duties. In other words, a civil service exam attempts to predict how successful you will be. Questions cover such a broad area that they cannot be as minute and detailed as school exam questions.

In the public service similar kinds of work, or positions, are grouped together in one "class." This process is known as *position-classification.* All the positions in a class are paid according to the salary range for that class. One class title covers all of these positions, and they are all tested by the same examination.

B. FOUR BASIC STEPS

1) Study the announcement

How, then, can you know what subjects to study? Our best answer is: "Learn as much as possible about the class of positions for which you've applied." The exam will test the knowledge, skills and abilities needed to do the work.

Your most valuable source of information about the position you want is the official exam announcement. This announcement lists the training and experience qualifications. Check these standards and apply only if you come reasonably close to meeting them.

The brief description of the position in the examination announcement offers some clues to the subjects which will be tested. Think about the job itself. Review the duties in your mind. Can you perform them, or are there some in which you are rusty? Fill in the blank spots in your preparation.

Many jurisdictions preview the written test in the exam announcement by including a section called "Knowledge and Abilities Required," "Scope of the Examination," or some similar heading. Here you will find out specifically what fields will be tested.

2) Review your own background

Once you learn in general what the position is all about, and what you need to know to do the work, ask yourself which subjects you already know fairly well and which need improvement. You may wonder whether to concentrate on improving your strong areas or on building some background in your fields of weakness. When the announcement has specified "some knowledge" or "considerable knowledge," or has used adjectives like "beginning principles of..." or "advanced ... methods," you can get a clue as to the number and difficulty of questions to be asked in any given field. More questions, and hence broader coverage, would be included for those subjects which are more important in the work. Now weigh your strengths and weaknesses against the job requirements and prepare accordingly.

3) Determine the level of the position

Another way to tell how intensively you should prepare is to understand the level of the job for which you are applying. Is it the entering level? In other words, is this the position in which beginners in a field of work are hired? Or is it an intermediate or advanced level? Sometimes this is indicated by such words as "Junior" or "Senior" in the class title. Other jurisdictions use Roman numerals to designate the level – Clerk I, Clerk II, for example. The word "Supervisor" sometimes appears in the title. If the level is not indicated by the title, check the description of duties. Will you be working under very close supervision, or will you have responsibility for independent decisions in this work?

4) Choose appropriate study materials

Now that you know the subjects to be examined and the relative amount of each subject to be covered, you can choose suitable study materials. For beginning level jobs, or even advanced ones, if you have a pronounced weakness in some aspect of your training, read a modern, standard textbook in that field. Be sure it is up to date and has general coverage. Such books are normally available at your library, and the librarian will be glad to help you locate one. For entry-level positions, questions of appropriate difficulty are chosen – neither highly advanced questions, nor those too simple. Such questions require careful thought but not advanced training.

If the position for which you are applying is technical or advanced, you will read more advanced, specialized material. If you are already familiar with the basic principles of your field, elementary textbooks would waste your time. Concentrate on advanced textbooks and technical periodicals. Think through the concepts and review difficult problems in your field.

These are all general sources. You can get more ideas on your own initiative, following these leads. For example, training manuals and publications of the government agency which employs workers in your field can be useful, particularly for technical and professional positions. A letter or visit to the government department involved may result in more specific study suggestions, and certainly will provide you with a more definite idea of the exact nature of the position you are seeking.

III. KINDS OF TESTS

Tests are used for purposes other than measuring knowledge and ability to perform specified duties. For some positions, it is equally important to test ability to make adjustments to new situations or to profit from training. In others, basic mental abilities not dependent on information are essential. Questions which test these things may not appear as pertinent to the duties of the position as those which test for knowledge and information. Yet they are often highly important parts of a fair examination. For very general questions, it is almost impossible to help you direct your study efforts. What we can do is to point out some of the more common of these general abilities needed in public service positions and describe some typical questions.

1) General information

Broad, general information has been found useful for predicting job success in some kinds of work. This is tested in a variety of ways, from vocabulary lists to questions about current events. Basic background in some field of work, such as sociology or economics, may be sampled in a group of questions. Often these are principles which have become familiar to most persons through exposure rather than through formal training. It is difficult to advise you how to study for these questions; being alert to the world around you is our best suggestion.

2) Verbal ability

An example of an ability needed in many positions is verbal or language ability. Verbal ability is, in brief, the ability to use and understand words. Vocabulary and grammar tests are typical measures of this ability. Reading comprehension or paragraph interpretation questions are common in many kinds of civil service tests. You are given a paragraph of written material and asked to find its central meaning.

3) Numerical ability

Number skills can be tested by the familiar arithmetic problem, by checking paired lists of numbers to see which are alike and which are different, or by interpreting charts and graphs. In the latter test, a graph may be printed in the test booklet which you are asked to use as the basis for answering questions.

4) Observation

A popular test for law-enforcement positions is the observation test. A picture is shown to you for several minutes, then taken away. Questions about the picture test your ability to observe both details and larger elements.

5) Following directions

In many positions in the public service, the employee must be able to carry out written instructions dependably and accurately. You may be given a chart with several columns, each column listing a variety of information. The questions require you to carry out directions involving the information given in the chart.

6) Skills and aptitudes

Performance tests effectively measure some manual skills and aptitudes. When the skill is one in which you are trained, such as typing or shorthand, you can practice. These tests are often very much like those given in business school or high school courses. For many of the other skills and aptitudes, however, no short-time preparation can be made. Skills and abilities natural to you or that you have developed throughout your lifetime are being tested.

Many of the general questions just described provide all the data needed to answer the questions and ask you to use your reasoning ability to find the answers. Your best preparation for these tests, as well as for tests of facts and ideas, is to be at your physical and mental best. You, no doubt, have your own methods of getting into an exam-taking mood and keeping "in shape." The next section lists some ideas on this subject.

IV. KINDS OF QUESTIONS

Only rarely is the "essay" question, which you answer in narrative form, used in civil service tests. Civil service tests are usually of the short-answer type. Full instructions for answering these questions will be given to you at the examination. But in case this is your first experience with short-answer questions and separate answer sheets, here is what you need to know:

1) Multiple-choice Questions

Most popular of the short-answer questions is the "multiple choice" or "best answer" question. It can be used, for example, to test for factual knowledge, ability to solve problems or judgment in meeting situations found at work.

A multiple-choice question is normally one of three types—

- It can begin with an incomplete statement followed by several possible endings. You are to find the one ending which *best* completes the statement, although some of the others may not be entirely wrong.
- It can also be a complete statement in the form of a question which is answered by choosing one of the statements listed.
- It can be in the form of a problem – again you select the best answer.

Here is an example of a multiple-choice question with a discussion which should give you some clues as to the method for choosing the right answer:

When an employee has a complaint about his assignment, the action which will *best* help him overcome his difficulty is to

A. discuss his difficulty with his coworkers
B. take the problem to the head of the organization
C. take the problem to the person who gave him the assignment
D. say nothing to anyone about his complaint

In answering this question, you should study each of the choices to find which is best. Consider choice "A" – Certainly an employee may discuss his complaint with fellow employees, but no change or improvement can result, and the complaint remains unresolved. Choice "B" is a poor choice since the head of the organization probably does not know what assignment you have been given, and taking your problem to him is known as "going over the head" of the supervisor. The supervisor, or person who made the assignment, is the person who can clarify it or correct any injustice. Choice "C" is, therefore, correct. To say nothing, as in choice "D," is unwise. Supervisors have and interest in knowing the problems employees are facing, and the employee is seeking a solution to his problem.

2) True/False Questions

The "true/false" or "right/wrong" form of question is sometimes used. Here a complete statement is given. Your job is to decide whether the statement is right or wrong.

SAMPLE: A roaming cell-phone call to a nearby city costs less than a non-roaming call to a distant city.

This statement is wrong, or false, since roaming calls are more expensive.

This is not a complete list of all possible question forms, although most of the others are variations of these common types. You will always get complete directions for answering questions. Be sure you understand *how* to mark your answers – ask questions until you do.

V. RECORDING YOUR ANSWERS

Computer terminals are used more and more today for many different kinds of exams.

For an examination with very few applicants, you may be told to record your answers in the test booklet itself. Separate answer sheets are much more common. If this separate answer sheet is to be scored by machine – and this is often the case – it is highly important that you mark your answers correctly in order to get credit.

An electronic scoring machine is often used in civil service offices because of the speed with which papers can be scored. Machine-scored answer sheets must be marked with a pencil, which will be given to you. This pencil has a high graphite content which responds to the electronic scoring machine. As a matter of fact, stray dots may register as answers, so do not let your pencil rest on the answer sheet while you are pondering the correct answer. Also, if your pencil lead breaks or is otherwise defective, ask for another.

Since the answer sheet will be dropped in a slot in the scoring machine, be careful not to bend the corners or get the paper crumpled.

The answer sheet normally has five vertical columns of numbers, with 30 numbers to a column. These numbers correspond to the question numbers in your test booklet. After each number, going across the page are four or five pairs of dotted lines. These short dotted lines have small letters or numbers above them. The first two pairs may also have a "T" or "F" above the letters. This indicates that the first two pairs only are to be used if the questions are of the true-false type. If the questions are multiple choice, disregard the "T" and "F" and pay attention only to the small letters or numbers.

Answer your questions in the manner of the sample that follows:

32. The largest city in the United States is
    A. Washington, D.C.
    B. New York City
    C. Chicago
    D. Detroit
    E. San Francisco

1) Choose the answer you think is best. (New York City is the largest, so "B" is correct.)
2) Find the row of dotted lines numbered the same as the question you are answering. (Find row number 32)
3) Find the pair of dotted lines corresponding to the answer. (Find the pair of lines under the mark "B.")
4) Make a solid black mark between the dotted lines.

VI. BEFORE THE TEST

Common sense will help you find procedures to follow to get ready for an examination. Too many of us, however, overlook these sensible measures. Indeed, nervousness and fatigue have been found to be the most serious reasons why applicants fail to do their best on civil service tests. Here is a list of reminders:

- Begin your preparation early – Don't wait until the last minute to go scurrying around for books and materials or to find out what the position is all about.
- Prepare continuously – An hour a night for a week is better than an all-night cram session. This has been definitely established. What is more, a night a week for a month will return better dividends than crowding your study into a shorter period of time.
- Locate the place of the exam – You have been sent a notice telling you when and where to report for the examination. If the location is in a different town or otherwise unfamiliar to you, it would be well to inquire the best route and learn something about the building.
- Relax the night before the test – Allow your mind to rest. Do not study at all that night. Plan some mild recreation or diversion; then go to bed early and get a good night's sleep.
- Get up early enough to make a leisurely trip to the place for the test – This way unforeseen events, traffic snarls, unfamiliar buildings, etc. will not upset you.
- Dress comfortably – A written test is not a fashion show. You will be known by number and not by name, so wear something comfortable.
- Leave excess paraphernalia at home – Shopping bags and odd bundles will get in your way. You need bring only the items mentioned in the official notice you received; usually everything you need is provided. Do not bring reference books to the exam. They will only confuse those last minutes and be taken away from you when in the test room.
- Arrive somewhat ahead of time – If because of transportation schedules you must get there very early, bring a newspaper or magazine to take your mind off yourself while waiting.
- Locate the examination room – When you have found the proper room, you will be directed to the seat or part of the room where you will sit. Sometimes you are given a sheet of instructions to read while you are waiting. Do not fill out any forms until you are told to do so; just read them and be prepared.
- Relax and prepare to listen to the instructions
- If you have any physical problem that may keep you from doing your best, be sure to tell the test administrator. If you are sick or in poor health, you really cannot do your best on the exam. You can come back and take the test some other time.

VII. AT THE TEST

The day of the test is here and you have the test booklet in your hand. The temptation to get going is very strong. Caution! There is more to success than knowing the right answers. You must know how to identify your papers and understand variations in the type of short-answer question used in this particular examination. Follow these suggestions for maximum results from your efforts:

1) Cooperate with the monitor

The test administrator has a duty to create a situation in which you can be as much at ease as possible. He will give instructions, tell you when to begin, check to see that you are marking your answer sheet correctly, and so on. He is not there to guard you, although he will see that your competitors do not take unfair advantage. He wants to help you do your best.

2) Listen to all instructions

Don't jump the gun! Wait until you understand all directions. In most civil service tests you get more time than you need to answer the questions. So don't be in a hurry. Read each word of instructions until you clearly understand the meaning. Study the examples, listen to all announcements and follow directions. Ask questions if you do not understand what to do.

3) Identify your papers

Civil service exams are usually identified by number only. You will be assigned a number; you must not put your name on your test papers. Be sure to copy your number correctly. Since more than one exam may be given, copy your exact examination title.

4) Plan your time

Unless you are told that a test is a "speed" or "rate of work" test, speed itself is usually not important. Time enough to answer all the questions will be provided, but this does not mean that you have all day. An overall time limit has been set. Divide the total time (in minutes) by the number of questions to determine the approximate time you have for each question.

5) Do not linger over difficult questions

If you come across a difficult question, mark it with a paper clip (useful to have along) and come back to it when you have been through the booklet. One caution if you do this – be sure to skip a number on your answer sheet as well. Check often to be sure that you have not lost your place and that you are marking in the row numbered the same as the question you are answering.

6) Read the questions

Be sure you know what the question asks! Many capable people are unsuccessful because they failed to *read* the questions correctly.

7) Answer all questions

Unless you have been instructed that a penalty will be deducted for incorrect answers, it is better to guess than to omit a question.

8) Speed tests

It is often better NOT to guess on speed tests. It has been found that on timed tests people are tempted to spend the last few seconds before time is called in marking answers at random – without even reading them – in the hope of picking up a few extra points. To discourage this practice, the instructions may warn you that your score will be "corrected" for guessing. That is, a penalty will be applied. The incorrect answers will be deducted from the correct ones, or some other penalty formula will be used.

9) Review your answers

If you finish before time is called, go back to the questions you guessed or omitted to give them further thought. Review other answers if you have time.

10) Return your test materials

If you are ready to leave before others have finished or time is called, take ALL your materials to the monitor and leave quietly. Never take any test material with you. The monitor can discover whose papers are not complete, and taking a test booklet may be grounds for disqualification.

VIII. EXAMINATION TECHNIQUES

1) Read the general instructions carefully. These are usually printed on the first page of the exam booklet. As a rule, these instructions refer to the timing of the examination; the fact that you should not start work until the signal and must stop work at a signal, etc. If there are any *special* instructions, such as a choice of questions to be answered, make sure that you note this instruction carefully.

2) When you are ready to start work on the examination, that is as soon as the signal has been given, read the instructions to each question booklet, underline any key words or phrases, such as *least*, *best*, *outline*, *describe* and the like. In this way you will tend to answer as requested rather than discover on reviewing your paper that you *listed without describing*, that you selected the *worst* choice rather than the *best* choice, etc.

3) If the examination is of the objective or multiple-choice type – that is, each question will also give a series of possible answers: A, B, C or D, and you are called upon to select the best answer and write the letter next to that answer on your answer paper – it is advisable to start answering each question in turn. There may be anywhere from 50 to 100 such questions in the three or four hours allotted and you can see how much time would be taken if you read through all the questions before beginning to answer any. Furthermore, if you come across a question or group of questions which you know would be difficult to answer, it would undoubtedly affect your handling of all the other questions.

4) If the examination is of the essay type and contains but a few questions, it is a moot point as to whether you should read all the questions before starting to answer any one. Of course, if you are given a choice – say five out of seven and the like – then it is essential to read all the questions so you can eliminate the two that are most difficult. If, however, you are asked to answer all the questions, there may be danger in trying to answer the easiest one first because you may find that you will spend too much time on it. The best technique is to answer the first question, then proceed to the second, etc.

5) Time your answers. Before the exam begins, write down the time it started, then add the time allowed for the examination and write down the time it must be completed, then divide the time available somewhat as follows:

- If 3-1/2 hours are allowed, that would be 210 minutes. If you have 80 objective-type questions, that would be an average of 2-1/2 minutes per question. Allow yourself no more than 2 minutes per question, or a total of 160 minutes, which will permit about 50 minutes to review.
- If for the time allotment of 210 minutes there are 7 essay questions to answer, that would average about 30 minutes a question. Give yourself only 25 minutes per question so that you have about 35 minutes to review.

6) The most important instruction is to *read each question* and make sure you know what is wanted. The second most important instruction is to *time yourself properly* so that you answer every question. The third most important instruction is to *answer every question.* Guess if you have to but include something for each question. Remember that you will receive no credit for a blank and will probably receive some credit if you write something in answer to an essay question. If you guess a letter – say "B" for a multiple-choice question – you may have guessed right. If you leave a blank as an answer to a multiple-choice question, the examiners may respect your feelings but it will not add a point to your score. Some exams may penalize you for wrong answers, so in such cases *only,* you may not want to guess unless you have some basis for your answer.

7) Suggestions
   a. Objective-type questions
      1. Examine the question booklet for proper sequence of pages and questions
      2. Read all instructions carefully
      3. Skip any question which seems too difficult; return to it after all other questions have been answered
      4. Apportion your time properly; do not spend too much time on any single question or group of questions
      5. Note and underline key words – *all, most, fewest, least, best, worst, same, opposite,* etc.
      6. Pay particular attention to negatives
      7. Note unusual option, e.g., unduly long, short, complex, different or similar in content to the body of the question
      8. Observe the use of "hedging" words – *probably, may, most likely,* etc.
      9. Make sure that your answer is put next to the same number as the question
      10. Do not second-guess unless you have good reason to believe the second answer is definitely more correct
      11. Cross out original answer if you decide another answer is more accurate; do not erase until you are ready to hand your paper in
      12. Answer all questions; guess unless instructed otherwise
      13. Leave time for review

   b. Essay questions
      1. Read each question carefully
      2. Determine exactly what is wanted. Underline key words or phrases.
      3. Decide on outline or paragraph answer

4. Include many different points and elements unless asked to develop any one or two points or elements
5. Show impartiality by giving pros and cons unless directed to select one side only
6. Make and write down any assumptions you find necessary to answer the questions
7. Watch your English, grammar, punctuation and choice of words
8. Time your answers; don't crowd material

8) Answering the essay question

Most essay questions can be answered by framing the specific response around several key words or ideas. Here are a few such key words or ideas:

M's: manpower, materials, methods, money, management
P's: purpose, program, policy, plan, procedure, practice, problems, pitfalls, personnel, public relations

a. Six basic steps in handling problems:
   1. Preliminary plan and background development
   2. Collect information, data and facts
   3. Analyze and interpret information, data and facts
   4. Analyze and develop solutions as well as make recommendations
   5. Prepare report and sell recommendations
   6. Install recommendations and follow up effectiveness

b. Pitfalls to avoid
   1. *Taking things for granted* – A statement of the situation does not necessarily imply that each of the elements is necessarily true; for example, a complaint may be invalid and biased so that all that can be taken for granted is that a complaint has been registered
   2. *Considering only one side of a situation* – Wherever possible, indicate several alternatives and then point out the reasons you selected the best one
   3. *Failing to indicate follow up* – Whenever your answer indicates action on your part, make certain that you will take proper follow-up action to see how successful your recommendations, procedures or actions turn out to be
   4. *Taking too long in answering any single question* – Remember to time your answers properly

IX. AFTER THE TEST

Scoring procedures differ in detail among civil service jurisdictions although the general principles are the same. Whether the papers are hand-scored or graded by machine we have described, they are nearly always graded by number. That is, the person who marks the paper knows only the number – never the name – of the applicant. Not until all the papers have been graded will they be matched with names. If other tests, such as training and experience or oral interview ratings have been given, scores will be combined. Different parts of the examination usually have different weights. For example, the written test might count 60 percent of the final grade, and a rating of training and experience 40 percent. In many jurisdictions, veterans will have a certain number of points added to their grades.

After the final grade has been determined, the names are placed in grade order and an eligible list is established. There are various methods for resolving ties between those who get the same final grade – probably the most common is to place first the name of the person whose application was received first. Job offers are made from the eligible list in the order the names appear on it. You will be notified of your grade and your rank as soon as all these computations have been made. This will be done as rapidly as possible.

People who are found to meet the requirements in the announcement are called "eligibles." Their names are put on a list of eligible candidates. An eligible's chances of getting a job depend on how high he stands on this list and how fast agencies are filling jobs from the list.

When a job is to be filled from a list of eligibles, the agency asks for the names of people on the list of eligibles for that job. When the civil service commission receives this request, it sends to the agency the names of the three people highest on this list. Or, if the job to be filled has specialized requirements, the office sends the agency the names of the top three persons who meet these requirements from the general list.

The appointing officer makes a choice from among the three people whose names were sent to him. If the selected person accepts the appointment, the names of the others are put back on the list to be considered for future openings.

That is the rule in hiring from all kinds of eligible lists, whether they are for typist, carpenter, chemist, or something else. For every vacancy, the appointing officer has his choice of any one of the top three eligibles on the list. This explains why the person whose name is on top of the list sometimes does not get an appointment when some of the persons lower on the list do. If the appointing officer chooses the second or third eligible, the No. 1 eligible does not get a job at once, but stays on the list until he is appointed or the list is terminated.

X. HOW TO PASS THE INTERVIEW TEST

The examination for which you applied requires an oral interview test. You have already taken the written test and you are now being called for the interview test – the final part of the formal examination.

You may think that it is not possible to prepare for an interview test and that there are no procedures to follow during an interview. Our purpose is to point out some things you can do in advance that will help you and some good rules to follow and pitfalls to avoid while you are being interviewed.

What is an interview supposed to test?

The written examination is designed to test the technical knowledge and competence of the candidate; the oral is designed to evaluate intangible qualities, not readily measured otherwise, and to establish a list showing the relative fitness of each candidate – as measured against his competitors – for the position sought. Scoring is not on the basis of "right" and "wrong," but on a sliding scale of values ranging from "not passable" to "outstanding." As a matter of fact, it is possible to achieve a relatively low score without a single "incorrect" answer because of evident weakness in the qualities being measured.

Occasionally, an examination may consist entirely of an oral test – either an individual or a group oral. In such cases, information is sought concerning the technical knowledges and abilities of the candidate, since there has been no written examination for this purpose. More commonly, however, an oral test is used to supplement a written examination.

Who conducts interviews?

The composition of oral boards varies among different jurisdictions. In nearly all, a representative of the personnel department serves as chairman. One of the members of the board may be a representative of the department in which the candidate would work. In some cases, "outside experts" are used, and, frequently, a businessman or some other representative of the general public is asked to serve. Labor and management or other special groups may be represented. The aim is to secure the services of experts in the appropriate field.

However the board is composed, it is a good idea (and not at all improper or unethical) to ascertain in advance of the interview who the members are and what groups they represent. When you are introduced to them, you will have some idea of their backgrounds and interests, and at least you will not stutter and stammer over their names.

What should be done before the interview?

While knowledge about the board members is useful and takes some of the surprise element out of the interview, there is other preparation which is more substantive. It *is* possible to prepare for an oral interview – in several ways:

1) Keep a copy of your application and review it carefully before the interview

This may be the only document before the oral board, and the starting point of the interview. Know what education and experience you have listed there, and the sequence and dates of all of it. Sometimes the board will ask you to review the highlights of your experience for them; you should not have to hem and haw doing it.

2) Study the class specification and the examination announcement

Usually, the oral board has one or both of these to guide them. The qualities, characteristics or knowledges required by the position sought are stated in these documents. They offer valuable clues as to the nature of the oral interview. For example, if the job involves supervisory responsibilities, the announcement will usually indicate that knowledge of modern supervisory methods and the qualifications of the candidate as a supervisor will be tested. If so, you can expect such questions, frequently in the form of a hypothetical situation which you are expected to solve. NEVER go into an oral without knowledge of the duties and responsibilities of the job you seek.

3) Think through each qualification required

Try to visualize the kind of questions you would ask if you were a board member. How well could you answer them? Try especially to appraise your own knowledge and background in each area, *measured against the job sought*, and identify any areas in which you are weak. Be critical and realistic – do not flatter yourself.

4) Do some general reading in areas in which you feel you may be weak

For example, if the job involves supervision and your past experience has NOT, some general reading in supervisory methods and practices, particularly in the field of human relations, might be useful. Do NOT study agency procedures or detailed manuals. The oral board will be testing your understanding and capacity, not your memory.

5) Get a good night's sleep and watch your general health and mental attitude

You will want a clear head at the interview. Take care of a cold or any other minor ailment, and of course, no hangovers.

What should be done on the day of the interview?

Now comes the day of the interview itself. Give yourself plenty of time to get there. Plan to arrive somewhat ahead of the scheduled time, particularly if your appointment is in the fore part of the day. If a previous candidate fails to appear, the board might be ready for you a bit early. By early afternoon an oral board is almost invariably behind schedule if there are many candidates, and you may have to wait. Take along a book or magazine to read, or your application to review, but leave any extraneous material in the waiting room when you go in for your interview. In any event, relax and compose yourself.

The matter of dress is important. The board is forming impressions about you – from your experience, your manners, your attitude, and your appearance. Give your personal appearance careful attention. Dress your best, but not your flashiest. Choose conservative, appropriate clothing, and be sure it is immaculate. This is a business interview, and your appearance should indicate that you regard it as such. Besides, being well groomed and properly dressed will help boost your confidence.

Sooner or later, someone will call your name and escort you into the interview room. *This is it.* From here on you are on your own. It is too late for any more preparation. But remember, you asked for this opportunity to prove your fitness, and you are here because your request was granted.

What happens when you go in?

The usual sequence of events will be as follows: The clerk (who is often the board stenographer) will introduce you to the chairman of the oral board, who will introduce you to the other members of the board. Acknowledge the introductions before you sit down. Do not be surprised if you find a microphone facing you or a stenotypist sitting by. Oral interviews are usually recorded in the event of an appeal or other review.

Usually the chairman of the board will open the interview by reviewing the highlights of your education and work experience from your application – primarily for the benefit of the other members of the board, as well as to get the material into the record. Do not interrupt or comment unless there is an error or significant misinterpretation; if that is the case, do not hesitate. But do not quibble about insignificant matters. Also, he will usually ask you some question about your education, experience or your present job – partly to get you to start talking and to establish the interviewing "rapport." He may start the actual questioning, or turn it over to one of the other members. Frequently, each member undertakes the questioning on a particular area, one in which he is perhaps most competent, so you can expect each member to participate in the examination. Because time is limited, you may also expect some rather abrupt switches in the direction the questioning takes, so do not be upset by it. Normally, a board member will not pursue a single line of questioning unless he discovers a particular strength or weakness.

After each member has participated, the chairman will usually ask whether any member has any further questions, then will ask you if you have anything you wish to add. Unless you are expecting this question, it may floor you. Worse, it may start you off on an extended, extemporaneous speech. The board is not usually seeking more information. The question is principally to offer you a last opportunity to present further qualifications or to indicate that you have nothing to add. So, if you feel that a significant qualification or characteristic has been overlooked, it is proper to point it out in a sentence or so. Do not compliment the board on the thoroughness of their examination – they have been sketchy, and you know it. If you wish, merely say, "No thank you, I have nothing further to add." This is a point where you can "talk yourself out" of a good impression or fail to present an important bit of information. Remember, *you close the interview yourself.*

The chairman will then say, "That is all, Mr. ______, thank you." Do not be startled; the interview is over, and quicker than you think. Thank him, gather your belongings and take your leave. Save your sigh of relief for the other side of the door.

How to put your best foot forward

Throughout this entire process, you may feel that the board individually and collectively is trying to pierce your defenses, seek out your hidden weaknesses and embarrass and confuse you. Actually, this is not true. They are obliged to make an appraisal of your qualifications for the job you are seeking, and they want to see you in your best light. Remember, they must interview all candidates and a non-cooperative candidate may become a failure in spite of their best efforts to bring out his qualifications. Here are 15 suggestions that will help you:

1) Be natural – Keep your attitude confident, not cocky

If you are not confident that you can do the job, do not expect the board to be. Do not apologize for your weaknesses, try to bring out your strong points. The board is interested in a positive, not negative, presentation. Cockiness will antagonize any board member and make him wonder if you are covering up a weakness by a false show of strength.

2) Get comfortable, but don't lounge or sprawl

Sit erectly but not stiffly. A careless posture may lead the board to conclude that you are careless in other things, or at least that you are not impressed by the importance of the occasion. Either conclusion is natural, even if incorrect. Do not fuss with your clothing, a pencil or an ashtray. Your hands may occasionally be useful to emphasize a point; do not let them become a point of distraction.

3) Do not wisecrack or make small talk

This is a serious situation, and your attitude should show that you consider it as such. Further, the time of the board is limited – they do not want to waste it, and neither should you.

4) Do not exaggerate your experience or abilities

In the first place, from information in the application or other interviews and sources, the board may know more about you than you think. Secondly, you probably will not get away with it. An experienced board is rather adept at spotting such a situation, so do not take the chance.

5) If you know a board member, do not make a point of it, yet do not hide it

Certainly you are not fooling him, and probably not the other members of the board. Do not try to take advantage of your acquaintanceship – it will probably do you little good.

6) Do not dominate the interview

Let the board do that. They will give you the clues – do not assume that you have to do all the talking. Realize that the board has a number of questions to ask you, and do not try to take up all the interview time by showing off your extensive knowledge of the answer to the first one.

7) Be attentive

You only have 20 minutes or so, and you should keep your attention at its sharpest throughout. When a member is addressing a problem or question to you, give him your undivided attention. Address your reply principally to him, but do not exclude the other board members.

8) Do not interrupt

A board member may be stating a problem for you to analyze. He will ask you a question when the time comes. Let him state the problem, and wait for the question.

9) Make sure you understand the question

Do not try to answer until you are sure what the question is. If it is not clear, restate it in your own words or ask the board member to clarify it for you. However, do not haggle about minor elements.

10) Reply promptly but not hastily

A common entry on oral board rating sheets is "candidate responded readily," or "candidate hesitated in replies." Respond as promptly and quickly as you can, but do not jump to a hasty, ill-considered answer.

11) Do not be peremptory in your answers

A brief answer is proper – but do not fire your answer back. That is a losing game from your point of view. The board member can probably ask questions much faster than you can answer them.

12) Do not try to create the answer you think the board member wants

He is interested in what kind of mind you have and how it works – not in playing games. Furthermore, he can usually spot this practice and will actually grade you down on it.

13) Do not switch sides in your reply merely to agree with a board member

Frequently, a member will take a contrary position merely to draw you out and to see if you are willing and able to defend your point of view. Do not start a debate, yet do not surrender a good position. If a position is worth taking, it is worth defending.

14) Do not be afraid to admit an error in judgment if you are shown to be wrong

The board knows that you are forced to reply without any opportunity for careful consideration. Your answer may be demonstrably wrong. If so, admit it and get on with the interview.

15) Do not dwell at length on your present job

The opening question may relate to your present assignment. Answer the question but do not go into an extended discussion. You are being examined for a *new* job, not your present one. As a matter of fact, try to phrase ALL your answers in terms of the job for which you are being examined.

Basis of Rating

Probably you will forget most of these "do's" and "don'ts" when you walk into the oral interview room. Even remembering them all will not ensure you a passing grade. Perhaps you did not have the qualifications in the first place. But remembering them will help you to put your best foot forward, without treading on the toes of the board members.

Rumor and popular opinion to the contrary notwithstanding, an oral board wants you to make the best appearance possible. They know you are under pressure – but they also want to see how you respond to it as a guide to what your reaction would be under the pressures of the job you seek. They will be influenced by the degree of poise you display, the personal traits you show and the manner in which you respond.

ABOUT THIS BOOK

This book contains tests divided into Examination Sections. Go through each test, answering every question in the margin. At the end of each test look at the answer key and check your answers. On the ones you got wrong, look at the right answer choice and learn. Do not fill in the answers first. Do not memorize the questions and answers, but understand the answer and principles involved. On your test, the questions will likely be different from the samples. Questions are changed and new ones added. If you understand these past questions you should have success with any changes that arise. Tests may consist of several types of questions. We have additional books on each subject should more study be advisable or necessary for you. Finally, the more you study, the better prepared you will be. This book is intended to be the last thing you study before you walk into the examination room. Prior study of relevant texts is also recommended. NLC publishes some of these in our Fundamental Series. Knowledge and good sense are important factors in passing your exam. Good luck also helps. So now study this Passbook, absorb the material contained within and take that knowledge into the examination. Then do your best to pass that exam.

EXAMINATION SECTION

EXAMINATION SECTION
TEST 1

DIRECTIONS: Each question or incomplete statement is followed by several suggested answers or completions. Select the one that BEST answers the question or completes the statement. *PRINT THE LETTER OF THE CORRECT ANSWER IN THE SPACE AT THE RIGHT.*

1. It is the obligation of each employee to keep his department informed as to his correct name, address, and telephone number. Any change of address MUST be reported within 1.____

   A. 24 hours B. 2 days C. 3 days D. 1 week

2. When should an on-the-job accident to an employee be reported to his supervisor? 2.____

   A. Only if the injury is serious
   B. As soon as possible
   C. After he is treated at the authority clinic
   D. If compensation for injury is called for

3. The PROPER type of firefighting equipment to be used on an electrical fire is a 3.____

   A. soda-acid type extinguisher
   B. fire hose and water
   C. dry-chemical type extinguisher
   D. foam type extinguisher

4. Of the following, the BEST reason for conductors to be courteous to passengers is to 4.____

   A. discourage vandalism
   B. speed up train operations
   C. maintain good public relations
   D. assure passenger safety

5. The MAIN reason for the authority posting commercial advertisements in subway cars is to 5.____

   A. increase the income of the authority
   B. help passengers pass time pleasantly on long runs
   C. make the cars attractive
   D. inform the passengers about good products

6. Of the following, the BEST reason why an employee is required to give his supervisor a written report of an unusual occurrence immediately is that the 6.____

   A. report may be too lengthy if the employee has more time for writing it
   B. employee will not be as likely to forget to make the report
   C. supervisor can keep his reports up-to-date
   D. report will tend to be more accurate

7. During the rush hour, a passenger asks a platform conductor for directions. If the conductor is not sure of the right answer, he should 7.____

   A. tell the passenger to find a public telephone and call train information
   B. tell the passenger to take the next arriving train and ask that train's conductor
   C. give the passenger directions that he thinks are right as long as he thinks that the passenger is headed in the right direction
   D. tell the passenger he is not sure and suggest that the passenger wait until they can ask the conductor on the next arriving train for the information

8. If a group of teenagers in a subway car is behaving in a disorderly manner, the FIRST thing a conductor should do is to 8.____

   A. request the motorman to call the transit police
   B. eject this group from the train
   C. ask this group to quiet down
   D. refuse to leave the station until this group quiets down

Questions 9-11.

DIRECTIONS: Questions 9 through 11 are to be answered on the basis of the Accident Report below. Read this report carefully before answering the questions. Select your answers ONLY on the basis of this report.

ACCIDENT REPORT

On February 14, at 3:45 P.M., Mr. Warren, while on the top of a stairway at the 34th Street Station, realized the *D* train was in the station loading passengers. In his haste to catch the train, he forcefully ran down the stairs, pushing aside three other people also going down the stairs. Mr. Parker, one of the three people, lost his footing and fell to the bottom of the stairs. Working on the platform, I saw Mr. Parker lose his footing as a result of Mr. Warren's actions, and I immediately went to his aid. Station Supervisor Brown was attracted to the incident after a crowd had gathered. After 15 minutes, the injured man, Mr. Parker, got up and boarded a train that was in the station and, therefore, he was not hurt seriously.

R. Sands #3214
Conductor

9. Since accident reports should only contain facts, which of the following should NOT be put into the accident report? 9.____

   A. The incident took place at the 34th Street Station
   B. Mr. Parker was not hurt seriously
   C. The date that the report was written
   D. Mr. Sands went to the aid of the injured man

10. The title of the person submitting the report was 10.____

   A. Porter
   B. Assistant Station Supervisor
   C. Conductor
   D. Passenger

11. The TOTAL number of different persons mentioned in this report is 11.____

A. seven B. six C. five D. four

12. If an employee desires to find out what his general duties and responsibilities are, he should refer to the authority's 12.____

A. bulletins periodically issued by the operating divisions
B. schedule of working conditions
C. book of rules and regulations governing employees
D. labor relations manual

13. Of the following, the BEST reason for prohibiting the use of intoxicating liquor by employees while on duty is that it may 13.____

A. make them too active
B. make them too talkative
C. impair their job performance
D. cause them to become ill

14. If a conductor sees a passenger with his feet on a seat, the conductor should 14.____

A. tell the passenger he will call a transit patrolman
B. ignore the situation if the car is not crowded
C. stare at him until he puts his feet on the floor
D. ask the passenger to please put his feet down

Questions 15-18.

DIRECTIONS: Questions 15 through 18 are to be answered on the basis of the Bulletin printed below. Read this Bulletin carefully before answering the questions. Select your answers ONLY on the basis of this Bulletin.

<u>BULLETIN</u>

Rule 107(m) states, in part, that *Before closing doors, they (Conductors) must afford passengers an opportunity to detrain and entrain....*

Doors must be left open long enough to allow passengers to enter and exit from the train. Closing doors on passengers too quickly does not help to shorten the station stop and is a violation of the safety and courtesy which must be accorded to all our passengers.

The proper and effective way to keep passengers moving in and out of the train is to use the public address system. When the train is excessively crowded and passengers on the platform are pushing those in the cars, it may be necessary to close the doors after a reasonable period of time has been allowed. Closing doors on passengers too quickly is a violation of rules and will be cause for disciplinary action.

15. Which of the following statements is CORRECT about closing doors on passengers too quickly?
It 15.____

A. will shorten the running time from terminal to terminal
B. shortens the station stop but is a violation of safety and courtesy
C. does not help shorten the station stop time
D. makes the passengers detrain and entrain quicker

16. The BEST way to get passengers to move in and out of cars quickly is to 16.____

A. have the platform conductors urge passengers to move into doorways
B. make announcements over the public address system
C. start closing doors while passengers are getting on
D. set a fixed time for stopping at each station

17. The conductor should leave doors open at each station stop long enough for passengers to 17.____

A. squeeze into an excessively crowded train
B. get from the local to the express train
C. get off and get on the train
D. hear the announcements over the public address system

18. Closing doors on passengers too quickly is a violation of rules and is cause for 18.____

A. the conductor's immediate suspension
B. the conductor to be sent back to the terminal for another assignment
C. removal of the conductor at the next station
D. disciplinary action to be taken against the conductor

Questions 19-21.

DIRECTIONS: Questions 19 through 21 are to be answered SOLELY on the basis of the Bulletin printed below. Read this Bulletin carefully before answering the questions.

<u>BULLETIN</u>

Conductors assigned to train service are not required to wear uniform caps from June 1 to September 30, inclusive.

Conductors assigned to platform duty are required to wear the uniform cap at all times. Conductors are reminded that they must furnish their badge numbers to anyone who requests, same.

During the above-mentioned period, conductors may remove their uniform coats. The regulation summer short-sleeved shirts must be worn with the regulation uniform trousers. Suspenders are not permitted if the uniform coat is removed. Shoes are to be black but sandals, sneakers, suede, canvas, or two-tone footwear must not be worn.

Conductors may work without uniform tie if the uniform coat is removed. However, only the top collar button may be opened. The tie may not be removed if the uniform coat is worn.

19. Conductors assigned to platform duty are required to wear uniform caps 19.____

A. at all times except from June 1 to September 30, inclusive
B. whenever they are on duty
C. only from June 1 to September 30, inclusive
D. only when they remove their uniform coats

20. Suspenders are permitted only if conductors wear 20.____

A. summer short-sleeved shirts with uniform trousers
B. uniform trousers without belt loops
C. the type permitted by the authority
D. uniform coats

21. A conductor must furnish his badge number to 21.____

A. authority supervisors *only*
B. members of special inspection *only*
C. anyone who asks him for it
D. passengers *only*

22. As a train is leaving a station, the conductor notices a passenger being dragged along the platform with his leg caught in a door. 22.____
The FIRST action the conductor should take is to

A. pull the emergency cord
B. call the motorman on the public address system
C. yell to the platform conductor to pull the man away from the door
D. run to the car door holding this passenger and try to help him

23. If a conductor is about to close the door and he sees a passenger with a folded baby carriage hastening to get on the train, he should 23.____

A. tell the passenger that baby carriages are not allowed on trains
B. tell the passenger to hurry up
C. hold the doors open long enough to allow the passenger to get on
D. hold the doors open no longer than the required 10 seconds

24. An employee must notify his assignment desk or control office that he will be absent because of illness one hour before his reporting time so that 24.____

A. a substitute can be provided if necessary
B. he can be denied sick leave if his attendance record is poor
C. his reason for absence can be checked quickly
D. the timekeeper in the payroll section can be properly notified

25. Kennedy Airport and LaGuardia Airport are both located in Queens. 25.____
Of the following, the CORRECT statement regarding their locations is that

A. both Kennedy Airport and LaGuardia Airport are in the northern section of Queens
B. both Kennedy Airport and LaGuardia Airport are in the southern section of Queens
C. Kennedy Airport is in the southern section of Queens while LaGuardia Airport is in the northern section of Queens
D. Kennedy Airport is in the northern section of Queens while LaGuardia Airport is in the southern section of Queens

26. Madison Square Garden is at the same general location as 26.____

A. Pennsylvania Station
B. Rockefeller Center
C. Battery Park
D. Grand Central Station

27. A park located in the northeast corner of the Bronx is 27.____

A. St. Mary's Park
B. Van Cortlandt Park
C. Crotona Park
D. Pelham Bay Park

28. The Manhattan terminal of the Staten Island Ferry is located CLOSEST to 28.____

A. Washington Square Park
B. the Queensboro Bridge
C. the World Trade Center
D. Union Square

29. Two points of interest located in the Bronx are 29.____

A. the New York Aquarium and the Hall of Fame
B. Orchard Beach and the New York Botanical Garden
C. Van Cortlandt Park and Citi Field
D. City Island and Grant's Tomb

30. Of the following, the one which is located south of 42nd Street in Manhattan is the 30.____

A. Rockefeller Center
B. United Nations Assembly Building
C. Inwood Hill Park
D. Empire State Building

KEY (CORRECT ANSWERS)

1.	D	16.	B
2.	B	17.	C
3.	C	18.	D
4.	C	19.	B
5.	A	20.	D
6.	D	21.	C
7.	D	22.	A
8.	C	23.	C
9.	B	24.	A
10.	C	25.	C
11.	B	26.	A
12.	C	27.	D
13.	C	28.	C
14.	D	29.	B
15.	C	30.	D

TEST 2

DIRECTIONS: Each question or incomplete statement is followed by several suggested answers or completions. Select the one that BEST answers the question or completes the statement. *PRINT THE LETTER OF THE CORRECT ANSWER IN THE SPACE AT THE RIGHT.*

Questions 1-3.

DIRECTIONS: Questions 1 through 3 are to be answered on the basis of the following Directive. Read this Directive carefully before answering these questions. Select your answer ONLY on the basis of this Directive.

DIRECTIVE

When work trains having miscellaneous equipment (flat cars, crane cars, etc.) are in transit, the following flagging and safety instructions must be adhered to:

1. When flat cars are at the forward end of a train, the Flagman will station himself on the leading car. The Flagman will keep in constant communication with the Train Operator through the use of sound-powered telephones. If sound-powered telephones become defective and alternate means of communications are needed, the Command Center must be called for instructions. Positive communications must be maintained while the train is in motion. Any loss of communication will be a signal for the Train Operator to *Stop and Investigate.*

2. When flat cars are trailing, the Flagman will station himself on the rear of the last motor car in a position to view the trailing cars. Flagmen must observe that tail lights are illuminated at all times.

3. At all times when these trains are stopped for any reason, the Train Operator must sound two blasts of the whistle or horn before proceeding.

4. Safety demands that Train Operators and Flagmen investigate all causes of a train going into emergency, particularly when an employee is known to be riding a flat car.

5. Under no circumstances will an employee walk across a flat car while a train is in motion.

1. When flat cars are at the forward end of a work train, the Flagman will station himself 1.____

   A. at the rear of the last motor car
   B. on the trailing flat car
   C. on the leading flat car
   D. at the front of the first motor car

2. When a train with flat cars has stopped and the Train Operator wishes to proceed again, he MUST 2.____

   A. call the Command Center
   B. shout instructions to the Flagman
   C. check that the Flagman is using the correct signals
   D. sound two blasts of the whistle or horn

3. When there is a loss of positive communication between the Train Operator and the Flagman while the train is in motion, the Train Operator should 3.____

A. tell the Flagman to use his flashlight for flagging
B. stop the train and investigate the situation
C. tell the Flagman to use hand signals for flagging
D. put the train into emergency

4. A conductor earns $21.64 per hour. He is paid time and one-half for each hour worked over 40 hours per week. If a conductor works 44 hours in one week, his gross salary for that week is 4.____

A. $995.36 B. $995.44 C. $999.44 D. $999.84

Questions 5-12.

DIRECTIONS: Questions 5 through 12 are to be answered on the basis of the Weekday Train Schedule for the Dumont Line below. In answering these questions, refer ONLY to this schedule.

WEEKDAY TRAIN SCHEDULE - DUMONT LINE

	EASTBOUND					WESTBOUND		
Train #	Harvard Square Leave	Pleasure Plaza Leave	Harding Street Leave	Magic Mall Arr.	Magic Mall Lv.	Harding Street Leave	Pleasure Plaza Leave	Harvard Square Arrive
69	7:48	7:51	7:56	8:00	8:06	8:10	8:15	8:18
70	7:54	7:57	8:02	8:06	8:12	8:16	8:21	8:24
71	8:00	8:03	8:08	8:12	8:18	8:22	8:27	8:30
72	8:04	8:07	8:13	8:17	8:22	8:26	8:31	8:34
73	8:08	8:11	8:17	8:21	8:26	8:30	8:35	8:38
74	8:12	8:15	8:20	8:24	8:30	8:34	8:39	8:42
75	8:16	8:19	8:24	8:28	8:34	8:38	8:43	8:46
69	8:20	8:23	8:28	8:32	8:38	8:42	8:47	8:50
70	8:26	8:29	8:34	8:38	8:44	8:48	8:53	8:56

5. Train #70 is scheduled to leave Pleasure Plaza on its second westbound trip to Harvard Square at 5.____

A. 7:57 B. 8:21 C. 8:29 D. 8:53

6. The time it should take Train #74 to go from Harvard Square to Magic Mall is ______ minutes. 6.____

A. 8 B. 12 C. 18 D. 30

7. As shown on this schedule, the number of trains arriving at Magic Mall and standing there for less than 6 minutes before leaving is 7.____

A. 0 B. 2 C. 7 D. 9

8. The number of trains shown on the schedule having different train numbers is 8.____

A. 6 B. 7 C. 8 D. 9

9. Going towards Harvard Square, Train #71 is scheduled to leave Pleasure Plaza at 9.____

A. 8:03 B. 8:18 C. 8:27 D. 8:30

10. Passengers boarding at Harding Street and wishing to get to Harvard Square by 8:45 would have to board a train which is scheduled to leave Magic Mall no later than 10.____

A. 8:26 B. 8:30 C. 8:34 D. 8:38

11. Train #73 should leave Harding Street on its eastbound trip ______ minutes after leaving Harvard Square. 11.____

A. 7 B. 8 C. 9 D. 10

12. Due to door trouble, Train #72 (eastbound) is turned at Harding Street when it was scheduled to leave, and this operation takes 5 minutes.
Since the running time for the return trip back to Harvard Square is the same time as that for the eastbound trip, it should arrive back at Harvard Square at 12.____

A. 8:22 B. 8:27 C. 8:31 D. 8:39

13. If a train comes to a sudden stop and there is a delay in proceeding, the conductor should explain the reason for the delay to the passengers in order to 13.____

A. prevent them from blaming the train crew
B. prevent them from going on the track
C. keep them informed and calm
D. get them to help each other

14. Recently, the authority instituted a program of closing off the rear portion of subway trains between the hours of 8 P.M. and 4 A.M.
This was done MAINLY to 14.____

A. ease the job of the conductor
B. cut down on the number of people needed to operate trains
C. allow necessary repairs to be made in the closed-off cars
D. attempt to cut down on crime in the subways.

Questions 15-19.

DIRECTIONS: Questions 15 through 19 are to be answered on the basis of the Broad Street Line timetable printed on the next page. The numbers represent the total time (in minutes) that it takes the Broad Street Line local and express trains to travel from Frankford Avenue to the stations listed. The running times shown on the table include station-stop times. When answering these questions, use this timetable.

BROAD STREET LINE

Stations	Total Running Times, In Minutes	
	Local	Express
Frankford Avenue	-	-
Columbus Street	7	-
Overland Parkway	12 1/2	10
Victoria Boulevard	15	-
Market Street	17	14
Prince Street	24	-
Kings Avenue	28	-
Elizabeth Drive	33	28
Paradox Place	35	-
Del Prado Parkway	38 1/2	33
Monroe Avenue	44	-
McKinley Plaza	48	41

15. Both an express train and local train are standing in the Market Street Station. If both trains leave Market Street at the same time, how many minutes would a rider SAVE by using an express train in traveling to Del Prado Parkway? 15.____

A. 1 1/2 B. 2 1/2 C. 3 1/2 D. 4 1/2

16. If a Broad Street local train leaves Columbus Street at 8:10 P.M., it should arrive at Monroe Avenue at ______ P.M. 16.____

A. 8:22 B. 8:34 C. 8:41 D. 8:47

17. A passenger takes a local train from Columbus Street to Overland Parkway and then an express train from Overland Parkway to McKinley Plaza. Assuming no waiting time at any station, the TOTAL trip should take ______ minutes. 17.____

A. 36 1/2 B. 43 1/2 C. 46 1/2 D. 51 1/2

18. A Broad Street local leaves Frankford Avenue at 9:15 A.M. A Broad Street express leaves Frankford Avenue at 9:18 A.M. At what station will the express meet the local? 18.____

A. Overland Parkway B. Market Street
C. Elizabeth Drive D. Del Prado Parkway

19. A conductor on the Broad Street Line is scheduled to make three roundtrips on the local train between Frankford Avenue and McKinley Plaza with a 6-minute layover at these two terminal stations. What is the TOTAL running time, including time for layovers? ______ hours and ______ minutes. 19.____

A. 4; 30 B. 4; 36 C. 5; 18 D. 5; 24

20. A woman passenger complains to a platform conductor that a public telephone in the station is not working and that she lost 20 cents in trying to use it. The conductor should tell her to 20.____

A. contact the telephone subdivision of the maintenance of way department
B. complain to the railroad clerk on duty in the change booth
C. contact the telephone company for a refund
D. make a complaint to a transit patrolman

21. A transportation authority institutes a half-fare program on Sundays. The MAIN purpose for this type of program is to 21.____

A. decrease the number of riders on buses and trains on Sundays
B. get more people to use trains and buses on Sundays
C. encourage people to visit points of interest in the city
D. find out if the fare should also be reduced during the week

22. If a conductor reads a bulletin which he doesn't understand, the BEST thing for him to do is to 22.____

A. try to follow the directions in the bulletin as well as he can
B. discuss the bulletin with other conductors
C. ask the motorman of his train for an explanation
D. ask his supervisor what the bulletin means

23. In order to be granted a paid or unpaid leave of absence on account of illness, an employee MUST file a written application, using the proper forms, within ______ after his return to work 23.____

A. 24 hours B. 2 days C. 3 days D. 1 week

24. A person has fallen on the subway station platform and says he has broken his leg. While waiting for an ambulance, the platform conductor should 24.____

A. help him over to a bench while putting as little weight as possible on the injured leg
B. make him as comfortable as possible without moving him
C. examine him for other possible injuries
D. apply a tourniquet to his leg from a first aid kit

25. Smoking in subway cars is prohibited MAINLY because it can 25.____

A. endanger a smoker's health
B. cause fires
C. bother passengers
D. cause cars to be littered with cigarette butts

KEY (CORRECT ANSWERS)

1. C
2. D
3. B
4. B
5. D
6. B
7. B
8. B
9. C
10. B
11. C
12. B
13. C
14. D
15. B
16. D
17. A
18. B
19. C
20. C
21. B
22. D
23. C
24. B
25. B

TEST 3

DIRECTIONS: Each question or incomplete statement is followed by several suggested answers or completions. Select the one that BEST answers the question or completes the statement. *PRINT THE LETTER OF THE CORRECT ANSWER IN THE SPACE AT THE RIGHT.*

1. Making an emergency stop of a subway train should be avoided if possible MAINLY because it might cause 1.____

   A. passengers to be late for work
   B. a train derailment
   C. hard wear on brakes and rails
   D. injuries to passengers

Questions 2-3.

DIRECTIONS: Questions 2 and 3 are to be answered SOLELY on the basis of the following Bulletin.

BULLETIN

Effective immediately, Conductors on trains equipped with public address systems shall make the following announcements in addition to their regular station announcement. At stations where passengers normally board trains from their homes or places of employment, the announcement shall be *Good Morning* or *Good Afternoon* or *Good Evening,* depending on the time of the day. At stations where passengers normally leave trains for their homes or places of employment, the announcement shall be *Have a Good Day* or *Good Night,* depending on the time of day or night.

2. The MAIN purpose of making the additional announcements mentioned in the Bulletin is MOST likely to 2.____

   A. keep passengers informed about the time of day
   B. determine whether the public address system works in case of an emergency
   C. make the passengers' ride more pleasant
   D. have the conductor get used to using the public address system

3. According to this Bulletin, a conductor should greet passengers boarding the *D* train at the Coney Island Station at 8 A.M. Monday by announcing 3.____

   A. Have a Good Day
   B. Good Morning
   C. Watch your step as you leave
   D. Good Evening

4. A passenger who seems to be drunk, but has not disturbed anyone, sits down on a seat near the conductor's cab. 4.____
   Of the following, the BEST way for the conductor to handle this situation is to

   A. gently lead this passenger off the train at the next station
   B. pay no attention to this passenger
   C. contact the transit police and ask them to remove this passenger
   D. do nothing but check frequently to see if this passenger starts to annoy anyone

5. Of the following, the BEST way for a conductor to keep informed of the latest changes in work procedures is to 5.____

   A. read all the new bulletins when he signs in
   B. study the book of rules
   C. ask the other conductors
   D. depend on his supervisor to tell him

6. The statistics compiled by the safety bureau of the subway system indicate that one out of every ten employees is qualified to give first aid and that one out of every five employees met with an accident during the past year. 6.____
   Of the following, the ONLY CORRECT statement that can be made from these figures for the past year is:

   A. One-half of the accidents occurred without a qualified employee present who was able to give first aid
   B. There would be fewer accidents if there were more employees trained to give first aid
   C. The number of accidents was twice the number of employees qualified to give first aid
   D. Each qualified employee gave first aid to two employees who had met with accidents

7. A conductor has just finished his tour of duty. As he is leaving the terminal, he finds a portion of the station platform has become slippery as a result of an oil spill. Which of the following is the BEST action for the conductor to take? 7.____

   A. Write a report to his supervisor about the condition of the platform.
   B. Warn any other employees that he sees before leaving about the condition of the platform.
   C. Report the condition of the platform to his supervisor when he sees him.
   D. Contact his supervisor about the condition of the platform before leaving the station.

8. While you are working as a conductor on a train, a friend of yours boards the train and tries to engage you in a long conversation. 8.____
   You should

   A. continue the conversation only between stations
   B. suggest that your friend talk to you only in the conductor's cab
   C. tell your friend that private conversations are not allowed while you are working
   D. request your friend to go into another car

9. An employee using his travel pass to ride the subway MUST 9.____

   A. report any unusual occurrences to his supervisor
   B. report it as stolen to the transit police if he loses it
   C. stand if there are not enough seats for revenue passengers
   D. notify the conductor that he is on the train and available for assistance in case of an emergency

10. Employers are often requested to arrange for *staggered working hours* for their employees in order to 10.____

A. increase the revenue obtained by the subway system
B. allow a husband and wife in a family to work different hours in order to care for the children
C. reduce rush hour crowding in the subways
D. give employees more time to shop when the department stores are open

11. The maximum number of cars which can be used on a subway train depends MAINLY on the 11.____

A. length of station platforms in the subway system
B. number of drive motors in each subway car
C. headway between trains during rush hours
D. number of matched pairs of new-type subway cars making up the train

12. If a platform conductor sees an armed robber *mugging* a passenger, he should 12.____

A. run up to the street and look for help
B. look for a weapon to attack the robber
C. call on other passengers to help him catch the robber
D. quickly contact the nearest transit patrolman

13. A *B* train which leaves Brighton Beach at 11:00 A.M. stops at 13.____

A. Prospect Avenue B. Union Street
C. 9th Street D. DeKalb Avenue

14. An express transfer station on the Lexington Avenue local is 14.____

A. 33rd Street B. Astor Place
C. 86th Street D. 96th Street

15. A passenger at the West 4th Street Station on the *A* line can transfer to the ______ line. 15.____

A. *L* B. *Q* C. *N* D. *F*

16. The BEST way to go to Grant's Tomb is by means of the ______ train. 16.____

A. *A* B. Number *1* C. Number *4* D. *D*

17. A passenger at the Coney Island-Stillwell Avenue Station on the *F* line wishes to transfer to the *A* line.
The NEAREST transfer point is 17.____

A. West 4th Street B. Church Avenue
C. Jay Street-MetroTech D. Bergen Street

18. An express station on the Number *3* line is 18.____

A. 50th Street
B. 59th Street-Columbus Circle
C. 72nd Street
D. Winthrop Street

19. The *G* train travels between Court Square and Church Avenue stations 19.____

A. all the time
B. at no time
C. during *rush* hours
D. during *off* hours

20. A passenger on the Number *1* Broadway local train can transfer FREE to the *A* train at which of the following stations? 20.____

A. Cathedral Parkway (110th Street)
B. 59th Street - Columbus Circle
C. Chambers Street
D. Penn Station - 34th Street

21. To visit the Cloisters, the BEST way is to a station on the ______ line. 21.____

A. *A*
B. Number *1*
C. Number *3*
D. *D*

22. A line that is in service during rush hours ONLY is the 22.____

A. *A* line
B. Franklin Ave. shuttle
C. *C* line
D. *E* line

23. A train that makes stops in Manhattan and the Bronx ONLY is the ______ train. 23.____

A. Number *1*
B. *B*
C. *F*
D. *J*

24. A train that makes stops ONLY in Manhattan is the ______ train. 24.____

A. *A*
B. *E*
C. *M*
D. None of the above

25. The *L* train is scheduled to travel from Rockaway Parkway to 8th Avenue in APPROXIMATELY ______ minutes. 25.____

A. 60
B. 50
C. 40
D. 25

KEY (CORRECT ANSWERS)

1. D
2. C
3. B
4. D
5. A
6. C
7. D
8. C
9. C
10. C
11. A
12. D
13. D
14. C
15. D
16. B
17. C
18. C
19. A
20. B
21. A
22. C
23. A
24. D
25. C

EXAMINATION SECTION
TEST 1

DIRECTIONS: Each question or incomplete statement is followed by several suggested answers or completions. Select the one that BEST answers the question or completes the statement. *PRINT THE LETTER OF THE CORRECT ANSWER IN THE SPACE AT THE RIGHT.*

1. A conductor's indication board indicates to the conductor of a MAXIMUM length train whether 1.____

   A. the motorman has stopped the train properly within the station platform limits
   B. the door trouble is electrical or mechanical
   C. any of his indication lights is malfunctioning
   D. his train is drummed properly

2. A conductor who finds that a public address system microphone is defective should 2.____

   A. notify the dispatcher immediately
   B. notify the desk trainmaster immediately
   C. try to repair the damage
   D. report it on the terminal car defect sheet

3. If a conductor operating a 10-car train with married pairs finds that he can no longer operate from the middle position, he must 3.____

   A. discharge the passengers
   B. operate from the 6th car
   C. operate from the 8th car
   D. call the tower

4. A conductor who is assigned to platform duty finds it necessary to leave his assigned post in an emergency. He should report that he is leaving his post to the nearest train dispatcher or the 4.____

   A. station supervisor
   B. desk trainmaster
   C. crew dispatcher
   D. platform conductor

5. When a conductor finds a firearm on a train or platform, the firearm must be 5.____

   A. personally delivered by the conductor to the lost property office
   B. sent to the most convenient location equipped with lost property bags
   C. turned over to the transit police
   D. forwarded by special messenger to the lost property office

6. If a motorman overruns the station platform, causing a few doors to be past the station platform, he should 6.____

   A. back up the train using the conductor as a flagman
   B. assist the conductor with the exiting passengers
   C. call the station department for instructions
   D. call the terminal train dispatcher for instructions

7. At a terminal, three amber (orange) lights are called ______ lights. 7.____

A. indication
B. gap
C. holding
D. starting

8. Four short blasts of a train horn means that the train 8.____

A. is answering a signal
B. crew needs assistance
C. is passing caution lights
D. is requesting a route or signal

9. An emergency telephone can be found by looking for a 9.____

A. red light
B. blue light
C. red and white sign
D. blue and white sign

10. If a train is approaching a river tube from which dense smoke is coming, the motorman should 10.____

A. ask the desk trainmaster whether he should enter the tube
B. discuss entering the tube with the conductor
C. not enter the tube under any condition
D. unload passengers immediately

11. In the event of a delay, the train crew must use the public address system, where provided, to inform the passengers.
The first announcement must occur within the first 10 minutes of the delay, and subsequent announcements must be made EVERY ______ minutes. 11.____

A. 2
B. 5
C. 10
D. 15

12. When a 10-car train is leaving the station, the conductor should observe the station platform until the train has moved ______ car length(s). 12.____

A. 1
B. 2
C. 3
D. 4

13. A succession of short blasts from a train horn could mean that the train 13.____

A. is making an irregular movement through the station
B. is answering a signal
C. needs a road car inspector
D. has vandals aboard

14. The train buzzer signal consisting of one long buzz 14.____

A. means stop
B. means proceed
C. is an answer to any signal
D. means that the train has vandals aboard

15. If a motorman loses indication after he has left the terminal, he should 15.____

A. immediately take the train out of service
B. travel at a reduced speed

C. keep the train in service only with the desk trainmaster's permission
D. keep the train in service if the conductor's indication is working

16. A no clearance area along the right of way is indicated by a sign that 16.____

A. has blue and white diagonal stripes
B. has blue and yellow diagnonal stripes
C. has red and white diagonal stripes
D. is all red

17. A motorman is LEAST likely to take orders from a 17.____

A. dispatcher
B. station supervisor
C. towerman
D. conductor

18. A conductor operating a train during non-rush hours discovers that he has a hanging guard light. 18.____
If he is unsuccessful when following the prescribed instructions for correcting the trouble, he should

A. ask the passengers to leave the train
B. notify the tower
C. direct the passengers to the good section of the train, and the defective section should then be isolated
D. stay in service only if he can get a road car inspector

19. Before a conductor leaves a train to go onto a station platform, he must FIRST 19.____

A. notify the nearest dispatcher
B. notify the desk trainmaster
C. open a conductor's emergency valve
D. open the train doors

20. The train buzzer signal consisting of two short buzzes 20.____

A. means stop
B. means proceed
C. is an answer to any signal
D. means that the motorman should signal for a road car inspector

21. If an end door is unlocked on an R-44 car, it is indicated by a lighted ______ light. 21.____

A. red B. blue C. yellow D. green

22. The train buzzer signal consisting of three short buzzes means that the 22.____

A. motorman should signal for a policeman
B. motorman should signal for a road car inspector
C. train has run by the station platform
D. motorman should signal for a signal maintainer

23. When an angry passenger asks for a conductor's badge number, the conductor should 23.____

A. make a report to the proper authorities
B. try to convince the passenger that he isn't at fault

C. try to get at the root of the problem
D. give his badge number without delay

24. When a conductor is assigned to a lay-up train, he has certain specified duties. The one that has the LOWEST priority is 24.____

A. removing discarded newspapers
B. closing all storm doors
C. closing all windows
D. closing all ventilators

25. If a certain conductor earns $540.00 a week and works 40 hours, his salary per hour is 25.____

A. $15.00 B. $12.75 C. $13.50 D. $14.25

26. A revenue train is a train that is used for 26.____

A. picking up money collected by railroad clerks
B. carrying passengers
C. collecting garbage
D. transporting lost articles

27. If a leader is ahead of schedule during rush hour, it is MOST likely that the follower will 27.____

A. have a lighter load of passengers than usual
B. not be affected
C. have a heavier load of passengers than usual
D. also be ahead of schedule

28. When a motorman on a local train fails to stop at a local station, the conductor should IMMEDIATELY 28.____

A. buzz the motorman
B. apply the hand brakes
C. open a conductor's emergency valve
D. notify the passengers

29. Of the following, the one that is NOT a required condition when trains are running on flooded tracks is that the 29.____

A. desk trainmaster must give permission
B. trains must run with extreme caution
C. water must be below the ball of the running rail
D. conductor must flag at the head of the train

30. When a train makes a stop at a station, the conductor MUST keep his doors open for at least ______ seconds. 30.____

A. 3 B. 5 C. 8 D. 10

31. A train is scheduled to leave the terminal at a certain time. The conductor must be at his operating position before this time by AT LEAST ______ minutes. 31.____

A. 2 B. 4 C. 6 D. 10

32. The remote control for the main car lights of a train operates from 32.____

A. 600 volts DC
B. 120 volts AC
C. a 32-volt battery
D. a 600-volt battery

33. If a passenger is observed on the tracks without permission, the FIRST thing a conductor should do is 33.____

A. call the police department
B. use the emergency alarm box
C. use the emergency telephone
D. sound the train horn

34. When power has been removed from a section of track, the only one authorized to restore it is the 34.____

A. desk trainmaster
B. man who removed the power
C. power department supervisor
D. safety officer

35. In the course of performing his duties, a conductor should have the LEAST need for 35.____

A. train schedules
B. general orders
C. train register sheets
D. work programs

36. When one contact shoe of a train car is touching the contact rail, the number of live shoes on that car is 36.____

A. 1 B. 2 C. 4 D. 8

37. In a ten-car train equipped with drum switches, the number of drum switches that must be in the OFF position when the train is in service is 37.____

A. 1 B. 2 C. 10 D. 20

38. In a ten-car train equipped with drum switches, the number of drum switches that should be in the THRU position when the train is in service is 38.____

A. 2 B. 10 C. 16 D. 20

39. A train buzzer signal will sound at locations where the drum switch is in the _______ position. 39.____

A. Full
B. Thru
C. Off
D. Release

40. Which of the following is not permitted on subway platforms and stairwells? 40.____

A. Talking on a cell phone
B. Touching subway signage
C. Assisting other riders with directions
D. Smoking cigarettes

41. When the motorman's indication is lit, it means that 41.____

A. all side doors are closed and locked
B. the conductor is getting indication
C. the train brake has been released
D. there is trouble in at least one of the train cars

42. The color of the motorman's indication is 42.____

A. red B. green C. white D. yellow

43. The color of the conductor's indication is 43.____

A. red B. green C. white D. yellow

44. When an exterior guard light on a train car is lit, it DEFINITELY means that 44.____

A. all doors are closed and properly locked
B. at least one door is not closed or properly locked
C. a door is being held open by a passenger
D. the doors on one side of the train car are closed and properly locked

45. When an interior guard light in a train car is lit, it DEFINITELY means that 45.____

A. all doors are closed and properly locked
B. at least one door is not closed or properly locked
C. a door is being held open by a passenger
D. the doors on one side of the train car are closed and properly locked

46. When a flagman moves a yellow flag up and down, it means that the motorman should 46.____

A. stop
B. call the tower
C. proceed very slowly
D. back up

47. The color of the caution lights that a flagman places on the side of the track is 47.____

A. red B. green C. white D. yellow

48. Conductors who are on duty are permitted to wear tinted glasses 48.____

A. in the tunnels after a physician has examined them
B. in the open, during daylight hours only
C. only if they also carry a pair of untinted glasses
D. at no time

49. Passengers must be removed from a train when the brakes are cut out on more than ______ of its cars. 49.____

A. 1 B. 1/5 C. 1/3 D. 1/4

50. The definition of *headway* is the 50.____

A. length of station stop time of a train
B. running time of a train
C. difference between the scheduled and actual time of a run
D. scheduled time interval between trains

KEY (CORRECT ANSWERS)

1.	A	11.	B	21.	B	31.	A	41.	A
2.	D	12.	C	22.	B	32.	C	42.	C
3.	A	13.	A	23.	D	33.	B	43.	A
4.	B	14.	A	24.	A	34.	A	44.	B
5.	C	15.	D	25.	C	35.	C	45.	B
6.	B	16.	C	26.	A	36.	C	46.	C
7.	D	17.	B	27.	C	37.	B	47.	D
8.	D	18.	C	28.	C	38.	C	48.	B
9.	B	19.	C	29.	D	39.	C	49.	C
10.	C	20.	C	30.	D	40.	D	50.	D

EXAMINATION SECTION
TEST 1

DIRECTIONS: Each question or incomplete statement is followed by several suggested answers or completions. Select the one that BEST answers the question or completes the statement. *PRINT THE LETTER OF THE CORRECT ANSWER IN THE SPACE AT THE RIGHT.*

Questions 1-16.

DIRECTIONS: Questions 1 through 16 are to be answered on the basis of the New York City subway system.

1. A man traveling on the number *4* train may change at Atlantic Avenue to the _______ train. 1.____

   A. *A* B. *F*
   C. number *6* D. number 2

2. An express station NOT on the *A* line is _____ Street. 2.____

   A. 160 B. 175 C. 181 D. 190

3. A *B* train which leaves Brighton Beach at 7:00 P.M. on Monday stops at 3.____

   A. Parkside Ave. B. Beverley Rd.
   C. Newkirk Plaza D. Avenue R

4. There is *D* train service to Coney Island 4.____

   A. at no time B. all the time
   C. during *off* hours D. during *rush* hours

5. The *R* train is scheduled to travel from Woodhaven Boulevard to Whitehall Street in APPROXIMATELY _______ minutes. 5.____

   A. 30 B. 40 C. 50 D. 70

6. During A.M. rush hours, Manhattan-bound number *1* trains may skip ______ Street. 6.____

   A. 157 B. 137
   C. 116 D. this train makes all stops

7. A passenger on the Lexington Avenue local can transfer free to the 6th Avenue local at 7.____

   A. 125 Street B. Hunts Pt. Ave.
   C. 96 Street D. Bleecker Street

8. The BEST way of going to the new Whitney Museum is by means of the 8.____

   A. Broadway Local B. Eighth Avenue Express
   C. Myrtle Ave. Express D. Culver Shuttle

9. The train that makes stops in three different boroughs is the ______ train. 9.____

   A. number *4* B. number *1* C. number 7 D. *C*

10. A line that terminates in Queens is the ______ line. 10.____

A. *D* B. *M* C. number *6* D. number *5*

11. A passenger on an *F* train should be able to get off at the Sutphin Blvd. station if the time is 11.____

A. 5 P.M. B. 6 P.M. C. 9 P.M. D. any time

12. The number 5 Lexington Ave. Express includes stops from Bronx Park East to Nereld Ave. 12.____

A. during rush hours only
B. at night only
C. at all times
D. on weekends only

13. A train that is NOT in service all the time is the 13.____

A. *E* train
B. Lexington Ave. Express
C. Franklin Ave. Shuttle
D. *C* train

14. The train which makes the MOST station stops between 59th St. and 125th St. in Manhattan is the ______ train. 14.____

A. *D* B. *A* C. *C* D. number *1*

15. On a Saturday, a passenger on the *A* train can transfer at 59th St.-Columbus Circle to the 15.____

A. *C* train
B. *D* train
C. *B* train
D. Flushing Local

16. On a Sunday, a passenger at the Times Square-42nd St. station can transfer from the ______ train to the ______ train. 16.____

A. *A; F*
B. *B; R*
C. number *7*; number *1*
D. *N; L*

Questions 17-21.

DIRECTIONS: Questions 17 through 21 are to be answered on the basis of the system of signal indications that is used on Division B (previously BMT and IND) and most of Division A (previously IRT).

17. A signal that gives ONLY a stop and stay indication is a(n) ______ signal. 17.____

A. marker B. dwarf C. automatic D. home

18. A signal whose aspect is controlled ONLY by the movement of a train is called a(n) ______ signal. 18.____

A. home B. automatic C. marker D. dwarf

19. The signal aspect which means proceed on main route and be prepared to stop at the next signal is ______ over ______. 19.____

A. green; green
B. yellow; green
C. green; yellow
D. yellow; yellow

20. The signal aspect which indicates that the motorman should stop and operate the automatic stop manual release is ______ over ______. 20.____

A. red; red
B. yellow; yellow
C. red; red over yellow
D. yellow; yellow over yellow

21. The signal aspect which means proceed is 21.____

A. white
B. yellow
C. blue
D. green

22. Triggers and closing caps are used for operating the doors of ______ car(s). 22.____

A. R-1 to R-14
B. R-15 to R-22
C. R-26 to R-38
D. the R-44

23. A conductor is required to report any change of address within ______ days. 23.____

A. two
B. three
C. five
D. seven

24. When a conductor finds that he cannot report for work because of illness, he is required to call in sick prior to reporting time by AT LEAST ______ hour(s). 24.____

A. 1
B. 2
C. 12
D. 24

25. A conductor must report absence due to illness to the 25.____

A. desk trainmaster
B. terminal dispatcher
C. motorman
D. crew dispatcher

26. The TOTAL number of interior and exterior guard lights on a train which is equipped with both types is 26.____

A. 1
B. 2
C. 4
D. 8

27. When there is smoke in the subway, a motorman should radio the 27.____

A. safety supervisor
B. desk trainmaster
C. ventilation supervisor
D. power department supervisor

28. The FIRST light that a flagman should place in its position when he is setting up is the ______ light. 28.____

A. red
B. green
C. white
D. yellow

29. Passengers on R-44 cars are alerted that the doors are being closed by means of a(n) 29.____

A. announcement over the PA system
B. buzzer
C. chime
D. flashing red light

30. The length of the R-44 car is APPROXIMATELY ______ feet. 30.____

A. 60 B. 65 C. 70 D. 75

KEY (CORRECT ANSWERS)

1. D	16. C
2. A	17. A
3. C	18. B
4. B	19. B
5. C	20. C
6. D	21. D
7. D	22. A
8. B	23. D
9. A	24. A
10. B	25. D
11. D	26. C
12. A	27. B
13. D	28. B
14. D	29. C
15. B	30. D

EXAMINATION SECTION
TEST 1

DIRECTIONS: Each question or incomplete statement is followed by several suggested answers or completions. Select the one that BEST answers the question or completes the statement. *PRINT THE LETTER OF THE CORRECT ANSWER IN THE SPACE AT THE RIGHT.*

1. Of the following, the MOST direct way of driving from Citi Field to Yankee Stadium would include using 1.____

   A. Northern Boulevard, the Queensborough Bridge, the Bruckner Expressway, and Fordham Road
   B. Northern Boulevard, the Third Avenue Bridge, and the Cross Bronx Expressway
   C. the Grand Central Parkway, the Triborough Bridge, and the Major Deegan Expressway
   D. the Grand Central Parkway, the Whitestone Expressway, the Bronx-Whitestone Bridge, and the Cross Bronx Expressway.

2. The one of the following which is CLOSEST to the Queensborough Bridge is 2.____

   A. 41st Street, Manhattan
   B. 59th Street, Manhattan
   C. 178th Street, Bronx
   D. Ferry Point Park, Bronx

3. A driver is going from Coney Island to Prospect Park. If he takes the most direct route, he will be traveling MOSTLY on 3.____

   A. Ocean Parkway
   B. the Shore Parkway
   C. Fort Hamilton Parkway
   D. the Prospect Expressway

4. Which one of the following leads MOST directly to the Throgs Neck Bridge? 4.____

   A. Hutchinson River Parkway
   B. Pelham Parkway
   C. Bruckner Expressway
   D. Clearview Expressway

5. At what corner of Central Park is Columbus Circle located? 5.____

   A. Northeast
   B. Northwest
   C. Southeast
   D. Southwest

6. When driving the most direct route from John F. Kennedy International Airport to LaGuardia Airport, you should use 6.____

   A. the Belt Parkway and the Brooklyn-Queens Expressway
   B. Southern Parkway and Ocean Parkway
   C. the Van Wyck Expressway and the Grand Central Parkway
   D. the Cross Island Parkway and the Clearview Expressway

7. Which one of the following passes CLOSEST to Belmont Park Race Track? 7.____

   A. Cross Island Parkway
   B. Southern Parkway
   C. Long Island Expressway
   D. Interborough Parkway

8. If a driver wishes to go from Battery Park to Long Island City, he would be LEAST likely to use the 8.____

A. Belt Parkway
B. Brooklyn Battery Tunnel
C. Manhattan Bridge
D. FDR Drive

9. City Island is a part of 9.____

A. Brooklyn B. Manhattan C. Queens D. the Bronx

10. The one of the following streets which runs parallel to and one block east of Central Park is ______ Avenue. 10.____

A. Madison B. Fifth C. Columbus D. Park

11. Of the following streets, the one which is CLOSEST to the Queens Borough Hall is 11.____

A. Atlantic Avenue
B. Queens Boulevard
C. Roosevelt Avenue
D. Woodhaven Boulevard

12. Which one of the following bridges connects the Bronx to Manhattan? The ______ Bridge. 12.____

A. Washington
B. Pelham
C. Williamsburg
D. Goethals

13. Which one of the following roads MOST NEARLY cuts through the middle of Staten Island in a generally north-south direction? 13.____

A. Richmond Avenue
B. Hylan Boulevard
C. Richmond Terrace
D. Henderson Avenue

14. Of the following, the MOST direct way of driving from Hunter College at 68th Street and Lexington Avenue, Manhattan to New York University at West 180th Street in the Bronx would include using the 14.____

A. FDR Drive, the Williamsburg Bridge, and the Bronx Pelham Parkway
B. FDR Drive, the Willis Avenue Bridge, and the Major Deegan Expressway
C. Henry Hudson Parkway, Dyckman Street, and the Mosholu Parkway
D. Henry Hudson Parkway, the Alexander Hamilton Bridge, and Westchester Avenue

15. Which one of the following streets is CLOSEST to both Brooklyn Marine Park and the Manhattan Bridge? ______ Avenue. 15.____

A. Flatbush B. Utica C. Atlantic D. New Lots

16. Of the following, the section of Brooklyn that is CLOSEST to Brownsville is 16.____

A. Bensonhurst
B. Brooklyn Heights
C. East New York
D. Red Hook

17. Lincoln Center for the Performing Arts is located 17.____

A. below 42nd Street
B. between Rockefeller Center and the UN Building
C. near Washington Square
D. west of Central Park

18. The current Madison Square Garden was built at 18.____

A. Columbus Circle
B. 8th Avenue and 50th Street
C. the site of Pennsylvania Station on 8th Avenue
D. the site of the former Steeplechase Park, on Surf Avenue in Coney Island

19. Which one of the following does NOT connect the Borough of Queens with The Bronx? ______ Bridge. 19.____

A. Throgs Neck
B. Triborough
C. Queensboro
D. Bronx-Whitestone

20. If you were planning to take a distinguished visitor on a tour of Uptown Manhattan, some of the highlights you would select would be 20.____

A. American Museum of Natural History, Hayden Planetarium, Gracie Mansion, Hunter College, and Grand Central Terminal
B. Central Park, Columbia University, Columbia-Presbyterian Medical Center, George Washington Bridge, and Metropolitan Museum of Art
C. Temple Emanu-El, Solomon R. Guggenheim Museum, Columbus Circle, Barnard College, and Port Authority Bus Terminal
D. Triborough Bridge, Lincoln Center for the Performing Arts, Cathedral of St. John the Divine, New York Hospital - Cornell Medical Center, and New York Botanical Gardens

21. If you were arranging an itinerary for a distinguished visitor that covered some of the highlights of Downtown Manhattan, you would select 21.____

A. Battery Park, Wall Street, City Hall, Chinatown, and Trinity Church
B. Brooklyn Bridge, Greenwich Village, New York University, New York Aquarium, and Grace Church
C. LaGuardia Airport, Bowling Green, Fulton Fish Market, St. Paul's Chapel, and Woolworth Building
D. Statue of Liberty, New York Stock Exchange, Woolworth Building, The Bowery, and Coney Island

22. If the itinerary you planned for a distinguished visitor were to cover some of the highlights of Midtown Manhattan, you would select 22.____

A. New York Public Library, Radio City Music Hall, Empire State Building, St. Thomas Church, and Manhattan College
B. Pennsylvania Station, Chrysler Building, Times Square, Carnegie Hall, and St. John's University
C. Rockefeller Center, United Nations, Metropolitan Opera House, Museum of Modern Art, and Madison Square Garden
D. United Nations, Rockefeller Center, Metropolitan Opera House, St. Patrick's Cathedral, and Hall of Fame for Great Americans

23. If you wished to escort a distinguished visitor on a tour of the City which included a hospital, the world's largest futures market, an exhibition hall, and the largest Gothic Cathedral in the world, you would take him to 23.____

A. Lenox Hill Hospital, American Stock Exchange, National Design Center, and Trinity Church
B. Mount Sinai Hospital, New York Cotton Exchange, New York Coliseum, The Cathedral of St. John the Divine
C. St. Vincent's Hospital, New York City Markets, Conference House, Riverside Church
D. The New York Hospital, New York Stock Exchange, Tea Center, and St. Patrick's Cathedral

24. If you planned to escort a distinguished visitor to the Cloisters, you would be taking him to a(n) 24.____

A. branch of the Metropolitan Museum of Art devoted to European medieval art and architecture
B. Off Broadway theatre notable for its avant-garde productions
C. restaurant specializing in Greek and Armenian dishes
D. supper club featuring jam sessions in modern jazz

25. Generally regarded as the oldest building in Manhattan, as well as a museum of revolutionary relics and Washington memorabilia, is 25.____

A. Fraunces Tavern
B. Jumel Mansion
C. Lefferts Homestead
D. Voorlezer's House

KEY (CORRECT ANSWERS)

1.	C	11.	B
2.	B	12.	A
3.	A	13.	A
4.	D	14.	B
5.	D	15.	A
6.	C	16.	C
7.	A	17.	D
8.	A	18.	C
9.	D	19.	C
10.	A	20.	B

21. A
22. C
23. B
24. A
25. A

TEST 2

DIRECTIONS: Each question or incomplete statement is followed by several suggested answers or completions. Select the one that BEST answers the question or completes the statement. *PRINT THE LETTER OF THE CORRECT ANSWER IN THE SPACE AT THE RIGHT.*

1. Grand Central Station is located in Manhattan at 1.____

   A. 34th Street and 7th Avenue
   B. Union Square
   C. Columbus Circle
   D. 42nd Street and Vanderbilt Avenue

2. Shea Stadium/Citi Field is located in 2.____

   A. Manhattan
   B. The Bronx
   C. Brooklyn
   D. Queens

3. The Empire State Building is located in Manhattan at 3.____

   A. Lenox Avenue and 125th Street
   B. Broadway and 42nd Street
   C. Fifth Avenue and 34th Street
   D. West 4th Street and Broadway

4. If a passenger asks you how to get to the Statue of Liberty, you should direct him to 4.____

   A. South Ferry
   B. the Verrazano Bridge
   C. the Port Authority Bus Terminal
   D. Penn Station

5. Lincoln Center for the Performing Arts is located in Manhattan at 5.____

   A. Broadway and 64th Street
   B. Central Park West and 86th Street
   C. Wall Street and Broadway
   D. 6th Avenue and 50th Street

6. City Hall is located NEAREST to 6.____

   A. South Ferry
   B. the Brooklyn Bridge
   C. Union Square
   D. Greenwich Village

7. The World Trade Center is located in 7.____

   A. The Bronx
   B. Brooklyn
   C. Manhattan
   D. Queens

8. Madison Square Garden is located 8.____

   A. in Central Park
   B. at Penn Station
   C. near Borough Hall
   D. at Coney Island

9. On which street in Manhattan is Macy's Department Store located? 9.____
______ Street.

A. 14th B. 34th C. 42nd D. 59th

10. Which of the following bridges is CLOSEST to City Hall? 10.____

A. Brooklyn
B. Williamsburg
C. 59th Street
D. George Washington

11. At which of the following is the New York Aquarium located? 11.____

A. Coney Island
B. South Ferry
C. Lincoln Center
D. Central Park

12. In which borough is Grand Central Terminal located? 12.____

A. The Bronx
B. Brooklyn
C. Manhattan
D. Queens

13. In which borough is Forest Hills located? 13.____

A. The Bronx
B. Brooklyn
C. Staten Island
D. Queens

14. In which borough is Yankee Stadium located? 14.____

A. The Bronx
B. Brooklyn
C. Manhattan
D. Queens

15. In which borough is Flatbush Avenue located? 15.____

A. The Bronx
B. Brooklyn
C. Manhattan
D. Queens

16. Times Square is located at the intersection of Broadway, Sixth Avenue, and ______ Street. 16.____

A. 14th B. 23rd C. 34th D. 42nd

17. There is NOT a direct subway route between 17.____

A. Queens and Brooklyn
B. Manhattan and The Bronx
C. Manhattan and Brooklyn
D. The Bronx and Queens

Questions 18-25.

DIRECTIONS: Questions 18 through 25 involve various places of interest in New York City. Column I lists the place of interest, while Column II lists four of the boroughs of New York City. For the question number involved, indicate the letter preceding the borough where the place of interest is located.

COLUMN I	COLUMN II	
18. New York Aquarium	A. Bronx	18.____
19. Carnegie Hall	B. Brooklyn	19.____
20. Citi Field	C. Manhattan	20.____
21. Lincoln Center	D. Queens	21.____
22. Sheepshead Bay		22.____
23. Van Cortlandt Park		23.____
24. LaGuardia Airport		24.____
25. Union Square		25.____

KEY (CORRECT ANSWERS)

1. D
2. D
3. C
4. A
5. A

6. B
7. C
8. B
9. B
10. A

11. A
12. C
13. D
14. A
15. B

16. D
17. D
18. B
19. C
20. D

21. C
22. B
23. A
24. D
25. C

READING COMPREHENSION
UNDERSTANDING AND INTERPRETING WRITTEN MATERIAL

EXAMINATION SECTION
TEST 1

DIRECTIONS: Each question or Incomplete statement is followed by several suggested answers or completions. Select the one that BEST answers the question or completes the statement. *PRINT THE LETTER OF THE CORRECT ANSWER IN THE SPACE AT THE RIGHT.*

Questions 1-10.

DIRECTIONS: Questions 1 through 10 are to be answered on the basis of the description of an incident given below. Read the description carefully before answering these questions.

DESCRIPTION OF INCIDENT

On Tuesday, October 8, at about 4:00 P.M., bus operator Sam Bell, Badge No. 3871, whose accident record was perfect, was operating his half-filled bus, No. 4392Y, northbound and on schedule along Dean Street. At this time, a male passenger who was apparently intoxicated started to yell and to use loud and profane language. The bus driver told this passenger to be quiet or to get off the bus. The passenger said that he would not be quiet but indicated that he wanted to get off the bus by moving toward the front door exit. When he reached the front of the bus, which at the time was in motion, the intoxicated passenger slapped the bus operator on the back and pulled the steering wheel sharply. This action caused the bus to sideswipe a passenger automobile coming from the opposite direction before the operator could stop the bus. The sideswiped car was a red 2007 Pontiac 2-door convertible, License 6416-KN, driven by Albert Holt. The bus driver kept the doors of his bus closed and blew the horn vigorously. The horn blowing was quickly answered as Sergeant Henry Burns, Badge No. 1208, and Patrolman Joe Cross, Badge No. 24643, happened to be following a few cars behind the bus in police car No. 736. The intoxicated passenger, who gave his name as John Doe, was placed under arrest, and Patrolman Cross took the names of witnesses while Sergeant Burns recorded the necessary vehicular information. Investigation showed that no one was injured in the accident and that the entire damage to the automobile was having its side slightly pushed in.

1. From the information given, it can be reasoned that 1.____

   A. it was just beginning to rain
   B. Dean Street is a two-way street
   C. there were mostly women shoppers on the bus
   D. most seats in the bus were filled

2. The name of the policeman who was riding in the police car with the sergeant was 2.____

   A. Cross B. Bell C. Holt D. Burns

3. From the description, it is evident that the passenger automobile was traveling 3.____

A. north B. south C. east D. west

4. It is logical to conclude that the passenger automobile was damaged on its 4.____

A. front end B. rear end
C. right side D. left side

5. A fact concerning the intoxicated passenger that is clearly stated in the above description is that he 5.____

A. was intoxicated when he got on the bus
B. hit a fellow passenger
C. pulled the steering wheel sharply
D. was not arrested

6. The bus operator called the attention of the police by 6.____

A. sideswiping an oncoming car
B. yelling and using profane language
C. blowing his horn vigorously
D. stopping a police car coming from the opposite direction

7. A reasonable conclusion that can be drawn from the above description is that 7.____

A. the name John Doe was fictitious
B. the sideswiped automobile was from out of town
C. some of the passengers on the bus were injured
D. the bus operator tried to put the intoxicated passenger off the bus

8. The number of the police car involved in the incident was 8.____

A. 4392Y B. 6416-KN C. 1208 D. 736

9. From the facts stated, it is obvious that the bus operator was 9.____

A. behind schedule
B. driving too close to the center of the street
C. discourteous to the intoxicated passenger
D. a good driver

10. It is clearly stated that the 10.____

A. sideswiped automobile was a blue sedan
B. bus driver kept the bus doors closed until the police came
C. incident happened on a Thursday
D. police sergeant took down the names of witnesses

Questions 11-20.

DIRECTIONS: Questions 11 through 20 are to be answered on the basis of the paragraph below covering cleaning supplies. Refer to this paragraph when answering these questions.

CLEANING SUPPLIES

Certain amounts of cleaning supplies are used each week at each station of the Transit Authority. The following information applies to a station of average size. For cleaning floors, tiles, and toilets, approximately 14 pounds of soap powder is used each week. A scouring powder is used to clean unusually difficult stains, and approximately 1 1/2 pounds is used in a week. A disinfectant solution is used for cleaning telephone alcoves, toilets, and booth floors, and approximately 1 quart of undiluted disinfectant is used each week. To make a regular strength disinfectant solution, 1/4 ounce of undiluted disinfectant is added to 14 gallons of water. One pint of lemon oil is used each week to polish metal surfaces in booths and in other station areas.

11. In a period of 4 weeks, the amount of soap powder that is used at the average station is MOST NEARLY _______ pounds. 11._____

    A. 48 B. 52 C. 56 D. 60

12. In a period of 1 year, the amount of scouring powder that is used at the average station is MOST NEARLY _______ pounds. 12._____

    A. 26 B. 52 C. 64 D. 78

13. If a certain large station uses 1 1/2 times the soap powder that an average station uses, then the larger station uses MOST NEARLY _______ pounds a week. 13._____

    A. 14 B. 21 C. 24 D. 28

14. To make a regular strength disinfectant solution, the number of ounces of undiluted disinfectant that should be added to 3 gallons of water is 14._____

    A. 4 B. 3/4 C. 1 D. 1 1/4

15. To make a double strength disinfectant solution, the number of ounces of undiluted disinfectant that should be added to 3 gallons of water is 15._____

    A. 4 B. 3/4 C. 1 D. 1 1/2

16. In a period of 4 weeks, the amount of lemon oil that is used at the average station is _______ gallon(s). 16._____

    A. 1/4 B. 4 C. 1 D. 1 1/2

17. In a period of one year, the amount of soap powder that is used at 5 average stations is MOST NEARLY _______ pounds. 17._____

    A. 260 B. 728 C. 3,640 D. 5,260

18. To clean a station that is difficult to remove, it would be BEST for a porter to use 18._____

    A. soap powder
    B. scouring powder
    C. disinfectant solution
    D. lemon oil

19. Lemon oil should be used for 19.____

A. scouring
B. regular cleaning
C. polishing metal surfaces
D. disinfecting

20. If a smaller than average station uses 3/4 of the amount of scouring powder than an average station uses, then in one week the amount of scouring powder used at the smaller station is MOST NEARLY ______ pound(s). 20.____

A. 7/8 B. 1 C. 1 1/8 D. I 1/4

Questions 21-25.

DIRECTIONS: Questions 21 through 25, inclusive, are to be answered on the basis of the bus cleaning instructions below, which should be performed in the order given. Read the instructions carefully before answering these questions.

1. SPRAY wheels and mud guards with hand water hose to remove loose dirt.
2. SCRUB mud guards with brush and cleaner.
3. SCRUB wheels with brush and cleaner.
4. SCRAPE grease from wheels with hand scraper.
5. RINSE wheels and mud guards with hand water hose.

21. The cleaning instructions which involve the same parts of the bus are 21.____

A. 1 and 2 B. 1 and 3 C. 2 and 4 D. 1 and 5

22. The scraping takes place 22.____

A. *after* both the spraying and rinsing
B. *after* the rinsing but before the scrubbing
C. *before* both the scrubbing and rinsing
D. *before* the rinsing but after the spraying

23. The hand water hose is NOT used to remove the grease because water 23.____

A. cannot remove the grease properly
B. would injure the motor
C. has to be used as cleaner solution
D. is used only for spraying

24. The brush is used in connection with operations 24.____

A. 1 and 2 B. 2 and 3 C. 3 and 4 D. 4 and 5

25. Loose dirt is removed by 25.____

A. scraping B. scrubbing C. spraying D. rinsing

KEY (CORRECT ANSWERS)

1. B
2. A
3. B
4. D
5. C

6. C
7. A
8. D
9. D
10. B

11. C
12. D
13. B
14. A
15. C

16. B
17. C
18. B
19. C
20. C

21. D
22. D
23. A
24. B
25. C

TEST 2

DIRECTIONS: Each question or incomplete statement is followed by several suggested answers or completions. Select the one that BEST answers the question or completes the statement. *PRINT THE LETTER OF THE CORRECT ANSWER IN THE SPACE AT THE RIGHT.*

Questions 1-8.

DIRECTIONS: Questions 1 through 8 are to be answered on the basis of the information contained in the safety rules given. Read these rules carefully before answering these questions.

<u>SAFETY RULES FOR EMPLOYEES WORKING ON TRACKS</u>

Always carry a hand lantern whenever walking a track and walk opposite to the direction of the traffic on that particular track, if possible.

At all times when walking track, take note of and be prepared to use the spaces available for safety, clear of passing trains. Be careful to avoid those positions where clearance is insufficient.

Employees are particularly cautioned with respect to sections of track on which regular operation of passenger trains may at times be abandoned and which are used as lay-up tracks. Such tracks are likely to be used at any and irregular times by special trains such as work trains, lay-up trains, etc. At no time can any section of track be assumed to be definitely out of service, and employees must observe, when on or near tracks, the usual precautions regardless of any assumption as to operating schedules.

1. Safety rules are MOST useful because they 1.____

   A. make it unnecessary to think
   B. prevent carelessness
   C. are a guide to avoid common dangers
   D. make the workman responsible for any accident

2. A trackman walking a section of track should walk 2.____

   A. to the left of the tracks
   B. to the right of the tracks
   C. in the direction of traffic
   D. opposite to the direction of traffic

3. One precaution a trackman should ALWAYS take is to 3.____

   A. have power turned off on those tracks where he is walking
   B. place a red lantern behind him when walking back
   C. wave his lantern constantly when walking track
   D. note nearby safety spaces

4. Special trains are GENERALLY 4.____

A. passenger trains on regular schedule
B. express trains on local tracks
C. work trains or lay-up trains
D. trains going opposite to traffic

5. A trackman walking track should 5.____

A. stay clear of all safety spaces
B. expect all trains to be on schedule
C. avoid tracks used by passenger trains
D. carry a hand lantern

6. On sections of track not used for regular passenger trains, a trackman should 6.____

A. follow the rules governing tracks in passenger train operation
B. assume that no trains will be operating
C. walk in the direction of traffic
D. disregard the usual precautions

7. Safety spaces are provided in the subway for 7.____

A. lay-up trains
B. passing trains
C. employee's use
D. easier walking

8. A trackman would NOT expect lay-up tracks to be used by 8.____

A. special trains
B. trains carrying passengers
C. work trains
D. lay-up trains

Questions 9-17.

DIRECTIONS: Questions 9 through 17 are to be answered on the basis of the porters' instructions given below. Read these instructions carefully before answering these questions

PORTERS' INSTRUCTIONS

Railroad porters are prohibited from entering the token booths except for cleaning or relieving the railroad clerk. When the cleaning or relief has been completed, porters must leave booths immediately and must not loiter in or around the booths. Porters must not leave their equipment or supplies, such as dust pans, brooms, soap, etc., on any stairway, passageway, walkway, or in any place which may result in a hazard to passengers or others. Whenever an accident occurs on the station where the porter is assigned, he must submit a report on the prescribed form, always giving the condition of the place where the accident occurred. Porters must be in prescribed uniforms ready for work when reporting *on* and *off* duty.

9. The instructions would indicate that the porters' PRINCIPAL duty is to 9.____

A. make out accident reports
B. wear a uniform
C. relieve the railroad clerk
D. keep the station clean

10. Porters are permitted to enter token booths 10.____

A. any time they wish
B. after finishing cleaning
C. to relieve the railroad clerk
D. to avoid loitering elsewhere

11. The PROBABLE reason why porters cannot stay in the token booth even if their regular work is done is because 11.____

A. they have a regular porters' room
B. they are not trusted
C. there is no room
D. passengers may complain

12. Porters are used to relieve railroad clerks MAINLY because 12.____

A. they need the training
B. they are conveniently available
C. their regular work is hard
D. their work is similar

13. In submitting a report on an accident, the porter is instructed to 13.____

A. explain the cause
B. use any convenient paper
C. give the condition of the place
D. telephone it to his superior

14. The MOST likely reason for having special uniforms for porters is to 14.____

A. give them authority
B. avoid a variety of unpresentable clothes
C. save them money
D. permit them to enter without paying fare

15. Evidently, porters must be careful where they leave their equipment or supplies to avoid 15.____

A. spoilage
B. theft
C. loss of time
D. injury to passengers

16. Such instructions to porters are NECESSARY because 16.____

A. there is no other way to do the work
B. it creates respect for authority
C. it avoids misunderstandings
D. they are not expected to think

17. A porter need NOT be in uniform when 17.____

    A. doing dirty work
    B. on his day off
    C. reporting *off* duty
    D. relieving the railroad clerk

Questions 18-25.

DIRECTIONS: Questions 18 through 25 are to be answered on the basis of the information contained in the safety rules given below. Read these rules carefully before answering these questions.

TRACKMEN SAFETY RULES ON EMERGENCY ALARM SYSTEM

In case of an emergency requiring the removal of high voltage power from the contact rail, any trackman seeing such emergency shall immediately operate the nearest emergency alarm box, and then immediately use the emergency telephone alongside the box to notify the trainmaster of the nature of the trouble. High voltage will be turned on again only by telephone order from an employee specifically having such authority. The location of this equipment along the trackway is indicated by a blue light. Trackmen are required to know the location of such boxes and the procedure to follow in order to have high voltage contact rail power removed on sections of elevated structure trackway which may not be equipped with emergency alarm boxes.

18. The location of an emergency alarm box is indicated by a(n) ______ light. 18.____

    A. red B. orange C. green D. blue

19. Operating an emergency alarm box 19.____

    A. calls the fire department
    B. removes power
    C. lights a blue light
    D. restores power

20. All trackmen 20.____

    A. have the authority to have power restored
    B. should know the location of emergency alarm boxes
    C. must call the trainmaster before operating an emergency alarm box
    D. do not have the right to operate an emergency alarm box

21. On a track having trains in operation, a nearby emergency alarm box would PROBABLY be operated if 21.____

    A. an employee cuts his hand
    B. the emergency telephone rings
    C. the blue light goes on
    D. a break is found in a running track rail

22. After operating an emergency alarm box, the trackman should use the emergency telephone immediately to speak to 22.____

A. his supervisor
B. the trainmaster
C. the station agent
D. his co-workers

23. It would be MOST important to have power restored as quickly as possible in order to reduce 23.____

A. power waste
B. train damage
C. train delays
D. fire hazard

24. If there are no emergency alarm boxes along a trackway, trackmen 24.____

A. cannot have power shut off
B. are not required to act in an emergency
C. can have power shut off by following the proper procedure
D. are forbidden to use the emergency telephone

25. On elevated structure trackways, 25.____

A. emergency alarm boxes may not be found
B. train delays never occur
C. the trainmaster is not notified on power removal
D. power is never removed

KEY (CORRECT ANSWERS)

1. C
2. D
3. D
4. C
5. D

6. A
7. C
8. B
9. D
10. C

11. A
12. B
13. C
14. B
15. D

16. C
17. B
18. D
19. B
20. B

21. D
22. B
23. C
24. C
25. A

TEST 3

DIRECTIONS: Each question or incomplete statement is followed by several suggested answers or completions. Select the one that BEST answers the question or completes the statement. *PRINT THE LETTER OF THE CORRECT ANSWER IN THE SPACE AT THE RIGHT.*

Questions 1-5.

DIRECTIONS: Questions 1 through 5 are to be answered on the basis of the paragraphs shown below covering the supply duties of assistant station supervisors. Refer to these paragraphs when answering these questions.

SUPPLY DUTIES OF ASSISTANT STATION SUPERVISORS

The assistant station supervisors on the 8 A.M. to 4 P.M. tour will be responsible for the ordering of porter cleaning supplies and will inventory individual stations under their jurisdiction in order to maintain the necessary supplies to insure proper sanitary standards. They will be responsible not only for the ordering of such supplies but will see to it that ordered supplies are distributed as required in accordance with order supply sheets. Assistant station supervisors on the 4 P.M. to 12 Midnight and 12 Midnight to 8 A.M. shift will cooperate with the A.M. station supervisor to properly control supplies.

The 4 P.M. to 12 Midnight assistant station supervisors will be responsible for the ordering and control of all stationery supplies used by railroad clerks in the performance of their duties. They will also see that supplies are kept in a neat and orderly manner. The assistant station supervisors in charge of *Supply Storerooms* will see to it that material so ordered will be given to the porters for delivery to the respective booths. Cooperation of all supervision applies in this instance.

The 12 Midnight to 8 A.M. assistant station supervisors will be responsible for the storing of materials delivered by special work train (sawdust, etc.). They will also see that all revenue bags which are torn, dirty, etc. are picked up and sent to the field office for delivery to the bag room.

Any supplies needed other than those distributed on regular supply days will be requested by submitting a requisition to the supply control desk for emergency delivery.

1. The assistant station supervisors who are responsible for ordering all stationery supplies used by railroad clerks are the ones on the ______ tour. 1.____

   A. 8 A.M. to 4 P.M.
   B. 4 P.M. to 12 Midnight
   C. 12 Midnight to 8 A.M.
   D. 4 P.M. to 2 P.M.

2. Storing of materials delivered by special work trains is the responsibility of assistant station supervisors on the ______ tour. 2.____

   A. 8 A.M. to 4 P.M.
   B. 4 P.M. to 12 Midnight
   C. 12 Midnight to 8 A.M.
   D. 4 P.M. to 2 P.M.

3. Torn revenue bags should be picked up and sent FIRST to 3.____

A. the bag room
B. the supply control desk
C. a supply storeroom
D. the field office

4. To obtain an emergency delivery of supplies on a day other than a regular supply day, a requisition should be submitted to the 4.____

A. appropriate zone office
B. appropriate field office
C. supply control desk
D. station supervisor

5. The assistant station supervisor responsible for ordering porter cleaning supplies will inventory individual stations PRIMARILY for the end purpose of 5.____

A. insuring proper sanitary standards
B. maintaining necessary supplies
C. keeping track of supplies
D. distributing supplies fairly

Questions 6-10.

DIRECTIONS: Questions 6 through 10 are to be answered on the basis of the paragraphs shown below entitled POSTING OF DIVERSION OF SERVICE NOTICES. Refer to these paragraphs when answering these questions.

POSTING OF DIVERSION OF SERVICE NOTICES

The following procedures concerning the receiving and posting of service diversion notices will be strictly adhered to:

Assistant station supervisors who receive notices will sign a receipt and return it to the Station Department Office. It will be their responsibility to ensure that all notices are posted at affected stations and a notation made in the transmittal logs. All excess notices will be tied and a notation made thereon, indicating the stations and the date notices were posted, and the name and pass number of the assistant station supervisor posting same. The word *EXCESS* is to be boldly written on bundled notices and the bundle placed in a conspicuous location. When loose notices, without any notations, are discovered in any field office, assistant station supervisor's office, or other Station Department locations, the matter is to be thoroughly investigated to make sure proper distribution has been completed. All stations where a diversion of service exists must be contacted daily by the assistant station supervisor covering that group and hour to ensure that a sufficient number of notices are posted and employees are aware of the situation. In any of the above circumstances, notation is to be made in the supervisory log. Station supervisors will be responsible for making certain all affected stations in their respective groups have notices posted and for making spot checks each day diversions are in effect.

6. An assistant station supervisor who has signed a receipt upon receiving service diversion notices must return the 6.____

A. notice to the Station Department office
B. receipt to the Station Department office
C. receipt and the transmittal log to the affected stations
D. transmittal log after making a notation in it

7. Of the following, the information which is NOT required to be written on a bundle of excess notices is the 7.____

A. names of the stations where the notices were posted
B. time of day when the notices were posted
C. date when the notices were posted
D. name and pass number of the assistant station supervisor posting the notices

8. If loose notices without notations on them are found, the situation should be investigated to make sure that the 8.____

A. notices are properly returned to the Station Department
B. assistant station supervisor responsible for the error is found
C. notices are correct for the diversion involved
D. notices have been distributed properly

9. To insure that employees are aware of a diversion in service, an assistant station supervisor covering the group and hour when a diversion exists must contact the involved stations 9.____

A. immediately after the diversion
B. on an hourly basis
C. on a daily basis
D. as often as possible

10. To make certain affected stations have notices posted when diversions occur, spot checks should be made by 10.____

A. station supervisors daily
B. station supervisors when necessary
C. assistant station supervisors daily
D. assistant station supervisors when necessary

Questions 11-15.

DIRECTIONS: Questions 11 through 15 are to be answered on the basis of the following paragraph entitled PROCEDURE FOR FLAGGING DISABLED TRAIN.

PROCEDURE FOR FLAGGING DISABLED TRAIN

If at any time it becomes necessary to operate a train from other than the forward cab of the leading car, a qualified Rapid Transit Transportation Department employee must be stationed on the forward end. The motorman and the aforesaid qualified employee must have a clear understanding as to the signals to be used between them as well as to the method of operation. They must know, by actual test, that they have communication between them. Flagging signals should be given at short intervals while train is in motion. If train is carrying passengers, they must be discharged at the next station. Motormen operating from other than the forward cab of the leading car must not advance the controller beyond the *series position*.

11. The qualified employee stationed at the forward end must NOT be a 11.____

A. motorman
B. conductor
C. motorman instructor
D. road car inspector

12. While the train is in motion, the employees stationed at the forward end should give a flagging signal 12.____

    A. at frequent intervals
    B. every time the train is about to pass a fixed signal
    C. only when he wants the train speed changed
    D. only when he wants to check his understanding with the motorman

13. Motormen operating from other than the leading car must NOT advance the controller beyond 13.____

    A. switching B. series C. multiple D. parallel

14. Considering the actual conditions on a passenger train in the subway, the MOST practical method of communication between the motorman and the employee at the forward end would be by using the 14.____

    A. train public address system
    B. buzzer signals
    C. whistle signals
    D. lantern signals

15. The BEST reason for discharging passengers at the next station under these conditions is that 15.____

    A. carrying passengers would cause additional delays
    B. it is not possible to operate safely
    C. the motorman cannot see the station stop markers
    D. the four lights at the front of the train will be red

Questions 16-25.

DIRECTIONS: **Questions 16 through 25, inclusive, are based on the description given in the following special assignment for a group of cleaners. Read the description carefully before answering these questions. Be sure to consider ONLY the information contained in these paragraphs.**

SPECIAL ASSIGNMENT

A special assignment of washing the ceilings and the tile walls of a number of stations on a particular line was given to a group of railroad cleaners. The stations included in the assignment were both local and express stations, and the only means of transferring between the uptown and the downtown trains without going to the street was to be found at the express stations. The stations to be cleaned were 2nd Street, 9th Street, 16th Street, 22nd Street, 29th Street, 36th Street, 44th Street, 52nd Street, 60th Street, and 69th Street. Of these, the express stations were located at 16th Street, 44th Street, and 69th Street.

Only the uptown sides of the stations were to be cleaned, as another gang was to clean the downtown sides. The cleaning operations were to start at 2nd Street and progress uptown. The materials furnished to perform this work consisted of pails, soap, long-handled brushes, mops, rags, and canvas covers for scales and vending machines.

The instructions were to scrub a surface first with a brush that had been immersed in a pail of soapy water, and then follow up by brushing with clear water. Any equipment on stations that was left uncovered and was splashed in the cleaning process was to be wiped clean with a rag.

16. The total number of different kinds of materials furnished to do the work of the special assignment was 16.____

A. 5 B. 6 C. 7 D. 8

17. Benches on station platforms were to be 17.____

A. moved out of the work area
B. covered with canvas
C. wiped clean with a rag if splashed
D. rinsed with clear water

18. Of the materials furnished, the instructions did NOT definitely call for the use of 18.____

A. mops B. brushes C. pails D. rags

19. The FIRST operation cleaners were instructed to do was to 19.____

A. clean walls with scouring cleanser
B. scrub ceilings with clear water
C. wipe vending machines clean with rags
D. scrub surfaces with soapy water

20. Furnished materials that were NOT used in the washing of ceilings included 20.____

A. soap B. pails C. rags D. water

21. Long-handled brushes were probably furnished because 21.____

A. ladders cannot be used on stations
B. such brushes are easier to handle than ordinary brushes
C. a better job can be done, since both hands are used
D. some areas could not be reached otherwise

22. Of the total number of stations included in the assignment, the number which were express stations was 22.____

A. 3 B. 7 C. 10 D. 20

23. A cleaner working in the *uptown* gang at 52nd Street Station was sent by his supervisor to get some supplies from the *downtown* gang which happened to be working at the same station. 23.____
The cleaner would have displayed good judgment if he

A. boarded a downtown train to 44th Street, crossed over, and then boarded an uptown train
B. descended to the tracks and crossed over cautiously
C. boarded an uptown train to 69th Street, crossed over, and then boarded a downtown train
D. went directly up to the street and crossed over

24. After finishing the assigned work at 44th Street, the men on this assignment were scheduled to go next to ______ Street. 24.____

A. 16th B. 36th C. 52nd D. 69th

25. A passenger at 29th Street wishing to transfer from a downtown local to an uptown local without paying an additional fare should transfer at ______ Street. 25.____

A. 44th B. 16th C. 36th D. 22nd

KEY (CORRECT ANSWERS)

1. B
2. C
3. D
4. C
5. A

6. B
7. B
8. D
9. C
10. A

11. D
12. A
13. B
14. B
15. A

16. B
17. C
18. A
19. D
20. C

21. D
22. A
23. D
24. C
25. B

READING COMPREHENSION
UNDERSTANDING AND INTERPRETING WRITTEN MATERIAL
EXAMINATION SECTION
TEST 1

DIRECTIONS Each question or incomplete statement is followed by several suggested answers or completions. Select the one that BEST answers the question or completes the statement. *PRINT THE LETTER OF THE CORRECT ANSWER IN THE SPACE AT THE RIGHT.*

Questions 1-8.

DIRECTIONS: Questions 1 through 8 are to be answered on the basis of the following regulations governing Newspaper Carriers when on subway trains or station platforms. These Newspaper Carriers are issued badges which entitle them to enter subway stations, when carrying papers in accordance with these regulations, without paying a fare.

<u>REGULATIONS GOVERNING NEWSPAPER CARRIERS WHEN ON SUBWAY TRAINS OR STATION PLATFORMS</u>

1. Carriers must wear badges at all times when on trains.
2. Carriers must not sort, separate, or wrap bundles on trains or insert sections.
3. Carriers must not obstruct platform of cars or stations.
4. Carriers may make delivery to stands inside the stations by depositing their badge with the station agent.
5. Throwing of bundles is strictly prohibited and will be cause for arrest.
6. Each bundle must not be over 18" x 12" x 15".
7. Not more than two bundles shall be carried by each carrier. (An extra fare to be charged for a second bundle.)
8. No wire to be used on bundles carried into stations.

1. These regulations do NOT prohibit carriers on trains from ______ newspapers. 1.____

   A. sorting bundles of
   B. carrying bundles of
   C. wrapping bundles of
   D. inserting sections into

2. A carrier delivering newspapers to a stand inside of the station MUST 2.____

   A. wear his badge at all times
   B. leave his badge with the railroad clerk
   C. show his badge to the railroad clerk
   D. show his badge at the newsstand

3. Carriers are warned against throwing bundles of newspapers from trains MAINLY because these acts may 3.____

   A. wreck the stand
   B. cause injury to passengers
   C. hurt the carrier
   D. damage the newspaper

4. It is permissible for a carrier to temporarily leave his bundles of newspapers 4.____

A. near the subway car's door
B. at the foot of the station stairs
C. in front of the exit gate
D. on a station bench

5. Of the following, the carrier who should NOT be restricted from entering the subway is the one carrying a bundle which is ______ long, ______ wide, and ______ high. 5.____

A. 15"; 18"; 18"
B. 18"; 12"; 18"
C. 18"; 12"; 15"
D. 18"; 15"; 15"

6. A carrier who will have to pay one fare is carrying ______ bundle(s). 6.____

A. one
B. two
C. three
D. four

7. Wire may NOT be used for tying bundles because it may be 7.____

A. rusty
B. expensive
C. needed for other purposes
D. dangerous to other passengers

8. If a carrier is arrested in violation of these regulations, the PROBABLE reason is that he 8.____

A. carried too many papers
B. was not wearing his badge
C. separated bundles of newspapers on the train
D. tossed a bundle of newspapers to a carrier on a train

Questions 9-12.

DIRECTIONS: Questions 9 through 12 are to be answered on the basis of the Bulletin printed below. Read this Bulletin carefully before answering these questions. Select your answers ONLY on the basis of this Bulletin.

BULLETIN

Rule 107(m) states, in part, that *Before closing doors they (Conductors) must afford passengers an opportunity to detrain and entrain...*

Doors must be left open long enough to allow passengers to enter and exit from the train. Closing doors on passengers too quickly does not help to shorten the station stop and is a violation of the safety and courtesy which must be accorded to all our passengers.

The proper and effective way to keep passengers moving in and out of the train is to use the public address system. When the train is excessively crowded and passengers on the platform are pushing those in the cars, it may be necessary to close the doors after a reasonable period of time has been allowed.

Closing doors on passengers too quickly is a violation of rules and will be cause for disciplinary actions.

9. Which of the following statements is CORRECT about closing doors on passengers too quickly? It 9.____

   A. will shorten the running time from terminal to terminal
   B. shortens the station stop but is a violation of safety and courtesy
   C. does not help shorten the station stop time
   D. makes the passengers detrain and entrain quicker

10. The BEST way to get passengers to move in and out of cars quickly is to 10.____

   A. have the platform conductors urge passengers to move into doorways
   B. make announcements over the public address system
   C. start closing doors while passengers are getting on
   D. set a fixed time for stopping at each station

11. The conductor should leave doors open at each station stop long enough for passengers to 11.____

   A. squeeze into an excessively crowded train
   B. get from the local to the express train
   C. get off and get on the train
   D. hear the announcements over the public address system

12. Closing doors on passengers too quickly is a violation of rules and is cause for 12.____

   A. the conductor's immediate suspension
   B. the conductor to be sent back to the terminal for another assignment
   C. removal of the conductor at the next station
   D. disciplinary action to be taken against the conductor

Questions 13-15.

DIRECTIONS: Questions 13 through 15 are to be answered on the basis of the Bulletin printed below. Read this Bulletin carefully before answering these questions. Select your answers ONLY on the basis of this Bulletin.

<u>BULLETIN</u>

Conductors assigned to train service are not required to wear uniform caps from June 1 to September 30, inclusive.

Conductors assigned to platform duty are required to wear the uniform cap at all times. Conductors are reminded that they must furnish their badge numbers to anyone who requests same.

During the above-mentioned period, conductors may remove their uniform coats. The regulation summer short-sleeved shirts must be worn with the regulation uniform trousers. Suspenders are not permitted if the uniform coat is removed. Shoes are to be black but sandals, sneakers, suede, canvas, or two-tone footwear must not be worn.

Conductors may work without uniform tie if the uniform coat is removed. However, only the top collar button may be opened. The tie may not be removed if the uniform coat is worn.

13. Conductors assigned to platform duty are required to wear uniform caps 13.____

A. at all times except from June 1 to September 30, inclusive
B. whenever they are on duty
C. only from June 1 to September 30, inclusive
D. only when they remove their uniform coats

14. Suspenders are permitted ONLY if conductors wear 14.____

A. summer short-sleeved shirts with uniform trousers
B. uniform trousers without belt loops
C. the type permitted by the authority
D. uniform coats

15. A conductor MUST furnish his badge number to 15.____

A. authority supervisors only
B. members of special inspection only
C. anyone who asks him for it
D. passengers only

Questions 16-17.

DIRECTIONS: Questions 16 and 17 are to be answered SOLELY on the basis of the following Bulletin.

<u>BULLETIN</u>

Effective immediately, Conductors on trains equipped with public address systems shall make the following announcements in addition to their regular station announcement. At stations where passengers normally board trains from their homes or places of employment, the announcement shall be *Good Morning* or *Good Afternoon* or *Good Evening,* depending on the time of the day. At stations where passengers normally leave trains for their homes or places of employment, the announcement shall be *Have a Good Day* or *Good Night,* depending on the time of day or night.

16. The MAIN purpose of making the additional announcements mentioned in the Bulletin is MOST likely to 16.____

A. keep passengers informed about the time of day
B. determine whether the public address system works in case of an emergency
C. make the passengers' ride more pleasant
D. have the conductor get used to using the public address system

17. According to this Bulletin, a conductor should greet passengers boarding the *D* train at the Coney Island Station at 8 A.M. Monday by announcing 17.____

A. Have a Good Day
B. Good Morning
C. Watch your step as you leave
D. Good Evening

Questions 18-25.

DIRECTIONS: Questions 18 through 25 are to be answered on the basis of the information regarding the incident given below. Read this information carefully before answering these questions.

INCIDENT

As John Brown, a cleaner, was sweeping the subway station platform, in accordance with his assigned schedule, he was accused by Henry Adams of unnecessarily bumping him with the broom and scolded for doing this work when so many passengers were on the platform. Adams obtained Brown's badge number and stated that he would report the matter to the Transit Authority. Standing around and watching this were Mary Smith, a schoolteacher, Ann Jones, a student, and Joe Black, a maintainer, with Jim Roe, his helper, who had been working on one of the turnstiles. Brown thereupon proceeded to take the names and addresses of these people as required by the Transit Authority rule which directs that names and addresses of as many disinterested witnesses be taken as possible. Shortly thereafter, a train arrived at the station and Adams, as well as several other people, boarded the train and left. Brown went back to his work of sweeping the station.

18. The cleaner was sweeping the station at this time because 18.____

A. the platform was unusually dirty
B. there were very few passengers on the platform
C. he had no regard for the passengers
D. it was set by his work schedule

19. This incident proves that 19.____

A. witnesses are needed in such cases
B. porters are generally careless
C. subway employees stick together
D. brooms are dangerous in the subway

20. Joe Black was a 20.____

A. helper B. maintainer
C. cleaner D. teacher

21. The number of persons witnessing this incident was 21.____

A. 2 B. 3 C. 4 D. 5

22. The addresses of witnesses are required so that they may later be 22.____

A. depended on to testify B. recognized
C. paid D. located

23. The person who said he would report this incident to the transit authority was 23.____

A. Black B. Adams C. Brown D. Roe

24. The ONLY person of the following who positively did NOT board the train was 24.____

A. Brown B. Smith C. Adams D. Jones

25. As a result of this incident, 25.____

A. no action need be taken against the cleaner unless Adams makes a written complaint
B. the cleaner should be given the rest of the day off
C. the handles of the brooms used should be made shorter
D. Brown's badge number should be changed

KEY (CORRECT ANSWERS)

1.	B	11.	C
2.	B	12.	D
3.	B	13.	B
4.	D	14.	D
5.	C	15.	C
6.	A	16.	C
7.	D	17.	B
8.	D	18.	D
9.	C	19.	A
10.	B	20.	B

21. C
22. D
23. B
24. A
25. A

TEST 2

DIRECTIONS: Each question or incomplete statement is followed by several suggested answers or completions. Select the one that BEST answers the question or completes the statement. *PRINT THE LETTER OF THE CORRECT ANSWER IN THE SPACE AT THE RIGHT.*

Questions 1-10.

DIRECTIONS: Questions 1 through 10 are to be answered on the basis of the information contained in the following safety rules. Read the rules carefully before answering these questions.

<u>SAFETY RULES</u>

Employees must take every precaution to prevent accidents, or injury to persons, or damage to property. For this reason, they must observe conditions of the equipment and tools with which they work, and the structures upon which they work.

It is the duty of all employees to report to their superior all dangerous conditions which they may observe. Employees must use every precaution to prevent the origin of fire. If they discover smoke or a fire in the subway, they shall proceed to the nearest telephone and notify the trainmaster giving their name, badge number, and location of the trouble.

In case of accidents on the subway system, employees must, if possible, secure the name, address, and telephone number of any passengers who may have been injured.

Employees at or near the location of trouble on the subway system, whether it be a fire or an accident, shall render all practical assistance which they are qualified to perform.

1. The BEST way for employees to prevent an accident is to 1.____

   A. secure the names of the injured persons
   B. arrive promptly at the location of the accident
   C. give their name and badge numbers to the trainmaster
   D. take all necessary precautions

2. In case of trouble, trackmen are NOT expected to 2.____

   A. report fires
   B. give help if they don't know how
   C. secure telephone numbers of persons injured in subway accidents
   D. give their badge number to anyone

3. Trackmen MUST 3.____

   A. be present at all fires
   B. see all accidents
   C. report dangerous conditions
   D. be the first to discover smoke in the subway

4. Observing conditions means to 4.____

A. look at things carefully
B. report what you see
C. ignore things that are none of your business
D. correct dangerous conditions

5. A dangerous condition existing on the subway system which a trackman should observe and report to his superior would be 5.____

A. passengers crowding into trains
B. trains running behind schedule
C. tools in defective condition
D. some newspapers on the track

6. If a trackman discovers a badly worn rail, he should 6.____

A. not take any action
B. remove the worn section of rail
C. notify his superior
D. replace the rail

7. The MAIN reason a trackman should observe the condition of his tools is 7.____

A. so that they won't be stolen
B. because they don't belong to him
C. to prevent accidents
D. because they cannot be replaced

8. If a passenger who paid his fare is injured in a subway accident, it is MOST important that an employee obtain the passenger's 8.____

A. name
B. age
C. badge number
D. destination

9. An employee who happens to be at the scene of an accident on a crowded station of the system should 9.____

A. not give assistance unless he chooses to do so
B. leave the scene immediately
C. question all bystanders
D. render whatever assistance he can

10. If a trackman discovers a fire at one end of a station platform and telephones the information to the trainmaster, he need NOT give 10.____

A. the trainmaster's name
B. the name of the station involved
C. his own name
D. the number of his badge

Questions 11-15.

DIRECTIONS: Questions 11 through 15 are to be answered on the basis of the information contained in the safety regulations given below. Refer to these rules in answering these questions.

REGULATIONS FOR SMALL GROUPS WHO MOVE FROM POINT TO POINT ON THE TRACKS

Employees who perform duties on the tracks in small groups and who move from point to point along the trainway must be on the alert at all times and prepared to clear the track when a train approaches without unnecessarily slowing it down. Underground at all times, and out-of-doors between sunset and sunrise, such employees must not enter upon the tracks unless each of them is equipped with an approved light. Flashlights must not be used for protection by such groups. Upon clearing the track to permit a train to pass, each member of the group must give a proceed signal, by hand or light, to the motorman of the train. Whenever such small groups are working in an area protected by caution lights or flags, but are not members of the gang for whom the flagging protection was established, they must not give proceed signals to motormen. The purpose of this rule is to avoid a motorman's confusing such signal with that of the flagman who is protecting a gang. Whenever a small group is engaged in work of an engrossing nature or at any time when the view of approaching trains is limited by reason of curves or otherwise, one man of the group, equipped with a whistle, must be assigned properly to warn and protect the man or men at work and must not perform any other duties while so assigned.

11. If a small group of men are traveling along the tracks toward their work location and a train approaches, they should 11.____

    A. stop the train
    B. signal the motorman to go slowly
    C. clear the track
    D. stop immediately

12. Small groups may enter upon the tracks 12.____

    A. only between sunset and sunrise
    B. provided each has an approved light
    C. provided their foreman has a good flashlight
    D. provided each man has an approved flashlight

13. After a small group has cleared the tracks in an area unprotected by caution lights or flags, 13.____

    A. each member must give the proceed signal to the motorman
    B. the foreman signals the motorman to proceed
    C. the motorman can proceed provided he goes slowly
    D. the last member off the tracks gives the signal to the motorman

14. If a small group is working in an area protected by the signals of a track gang, the members of the small group 14.____

    A. need not be concerned with train movement
    B. must give the proceed signal together with the track gang

C. can delegate one of their members to give the proceed signal
D. must not give the proceed signal

15. If the view of approaching trains is blocked, the small group should 15.____

A. move to where they can see the trains
B. delegate one of the group to warn and protect them
C. keep their ears alert for approaching trains
D. refuse to work at such locations

Questions 16-25.

DIRECTIONS: Questions 16 through 25 are to be answered SOLELY on the basis of the article about general safety precautions given below.

GENERAL SAFETY PRECAUTIONS

When work is being done on or next to a track on which regular trains are running, special signals must be displayed as called for in the general rules for flagging. Yellow caution signals, green clear signals, and a flagman with a red danger signal are required for the protection of traffic and workmen in accordance with the standard flagging rules. The flagman shall also carry a white signal for display to the motorman when he may proceed. The foreman in charge must see that proper signals are displayed.

On elevated lines during daylight hours, the yellow signal shall be a yellow flag, the red signal shall be a red flag, the green signal shall be a green flag, and the white signal shall be a white flag. In subway sections, and on elevated lines after dark, the yellow signal shall be a yellow lantern, the red signal shall be a red lantern, the green signal shall be a green lantern, and the white signal shall be a white lantern.

Caution and clear signals are to be secured to the elevated or subway structure with non-metallic fastenings outside the clearance line of the train and on the motorman's side of the track.

16. On elevated lines during daylight hours, the caution signal is a 16.____

A. yellow lantern
B. green lantern
C. yellow flag
D. green flag

17. In subway sections, the clear signal is a 17.____

A. yellow lantern
B. green lantern
C. yellow flag
D. green flag

18. The MINIMUM number of lanterns that a subway track flagman should carry is 18.____

A. 1
B. 2
C. 3
D. 4

19. The PRIMARY purpose of flagging is to protect the 19.____

A. flagman
B. motorman
C. track workers
D. railroad

20. A suitable fastening for securing caution lights to the elevated or subway structure is 20.____

A. copper nails
B. steel wire
C. brass rods
D. cotton twine

21. On elevated structures during daylight hours, the red flag is held by the 21.____

A. motorman B. foreman C. trackman D. flagman

22. The signal used in the subway to notify a motorman to proceed is a 22.____

A. white lantern
B. green lantern
C. red flag
D. yellow flag

23. The caution, clear, and danger signals are displayed for the information of 23.____

A. trackmen B. workmen C. flagmen D. motormen

24. Since the motorman's cab is on the right-hand side, caution signals should be secured to the 24.____

A. right-hand running rail
B. left-hand running rail
C. structure to the right of the track
D. structure to the left of the track

25. In a track work gang, the person responsible for the proper display of signals is the 25.____

A. track worker
B. foreman
C. motorman
D. flagman

KEY (CORRECT ANSWERS)

1.	D	11.	C
2.	B	12.	B
3.	C	13.	A
4.	A	14.	D
5.	C	15.	B
6.	C	16.	C
7.	C	17.	B
8.	A	18.	B
9.	D	19.	C
10.	A	20.	D

21. D
22. A
23. D
24. C
25. B

TEST 3

DIRECTIONS: Each question or incomplete statement is followed by several suggested answers or completions. Select the one that BEST answers the question or completes the statement. *PRINT THE LETTER OF THE CORRECT ANSWER IN THE SPACE AT THE RIGHT.*

Questions 1-6.

DIRECTIONS: Questions 1 through 6 are to be answered on the basis of the Bulletin Order given below. Refer to this bulletin when answering these questions.

<u>BULLETIN ORDER NO. 67</u>

SUBJECT: Procedure for Handling Fire Occurrences

In order that the Fire Department may be notified of all fires, even those that have been extinguished by our own employees, any employee having knowledge of a fire must notify the Station Department Office immediately on telephone extensions D-4177, D-4181, D-4185, or D-4189.

Specific information regarding the fire should include the location of the fire, the approximate distance north or south of the nearest station, and the track designation, line, and division.

In addition, the report should contain information as to the status of the fire and whether our forces have extinguished it or if Fire Department equipment is required.

When all information has been obtained, the Station Supervisor in Charge in the Station Department Office will notify the Desk Trainmaster of the Division involved.

Richard Roe,
Superintendent

1. An employee having knowledge of a fire should FIRST notify the 1.____

   A. Station Department Office
   B. Fire Department
   C. Desk Trainmaster
   D. Station Supervisor

2. If bulletin order number 1 was issued on January 2, bulletins are being issued at the monthly average of 2.____

   A. 8 B. 10 C. 12 D. 14

3. It is clear from the bulletin that 3.____

   A. employees are expected to be expert fire fighters
   B. many fires occur on the transit system
   C. train service is usually suspended whenever a fire occurs
   D. some fires are extinguished without the help of the Fire Department

4. From the information furnished in this bulletin, it can he assumed that the 4.____

A. Station Department office handles a considerable number of telephone calls
B. Superintendent Investigates the handling of all subway fires
C. Fire Department is notified only in ease of large fires
D. employee first having knowledge of the fire must call all 4 extensions

5. The PROBABLE reason for notifying the Fire Department even when the fire has been extinguished by a subway employee is because the Fire Department is 5.____

A. a city agency
B. still responsible to check the fire
C. concerned with fire prevention
D. required to clean up after the fire

6. Information about the fire NOT specifically required is 6.____

A. track B. time of day C. station D. division

Questions 7-10.

DIRECTIONS: Questions 7 through 10 are to be answered on the basis of the paragraph on fire fighting shown below. When answering these questions, refer to this paragraph.

FIRE FIGHTING

A security officer should remember the cardinal rule that water or soda acid fire extinguishers should not be used on any electrical fire, and apply it in the case of a fire near the third rail. In addition, security officers should familiarize themselves with all available fire alarms and fire-fighting equipment within their assigned posts. Use of the fire alarm should bring responding Fire Department apparatus quickly to the scene. Familiarity with the fire-fighting equipment near his post would help in putting out incipient fires. Any man calling for the Fire Department should remain outside so that he can direct the Fire Department to the fire. As soon as possible thereafter, the special inspection desk must be notified, and a complete written report of the fire, no matter how small, must be submitted to this office. The security officer must give the exact time and place it started, who discovered it, how it was extinguished, the damage done, cause of same, list of any injured persons with the extent of their injuries, and the name of the Fire Chief in charge. All defects noticed by the security officer concerning the fire alarm or any fire-fighting equipment must be reported to the special inspection department.

7. It would be PROPER to use water to put out a fire in a(n) 7.____

A. electric motor
B. electric switch box
C. waste paper trash can
D. electric generator

8. After calling the Fire Department from a street box to report a fire, the security officer should then 8.____

A. return to the fire and help put it out
B. stay outside and direct the Fire Department to the fire
C. find a phone and call his boss
D. write out a report for the special inspection desk

9. A security officer is required to submit a complete written report of a fire 9.____

A. two weeks after the fire
B. the day following the fire
C. as soon as possible
D. at his convenience

10. In his report of a fire, it is NOT necessary for the security officer to state 10.____

A. time and place of the fire
B. who discovered the fire
C. the names of persons injured
D. quantity of Fire Department equipment used

Questions 11-16.

DIRECTIONS: Questions 11 through 16 are to be answered on the basis of the Notice given below. Refer to this Notice in answering these questions.

NOTICE

Your attention is called to Route Request Buttons that are installed on all new type Interlocking Home Signals where there is a choice of route in the midtown area. The route request button is to be operated by the motorman when the home signal is at danger and no call-on is displayed or when improper route is displayed.

To operate, the motorman will press the button for the desiredroute as indicated under each button; a light will then go on over the buttons to inform the motorman that his request has been registered in the tower.

If the towerman desires to give the motorman a route other than the one he selected, the towerman will cancel out the light over the route selection buttons. The motorman will then accept the route given.

If no route or call-on is given, the motorman will sound his whistle for the signal maintainer, secure his train, and call the desk trainmaster.

11. The official titles of the two classes of employee whose actions would MOST frequently be affected by the contents of this notice are 11.____

A. motorman and trainmaster
B. signal maintainer and trainmaster
C. towerman and motorman
D. signal maintainer and towerman

12. A motorman should use a route request button when 12.____

A. the signal indicates proceed on main line
B. a call-on is displayed
C. the signal indicates stop
D. the signal indicates proceed on diverging route

13. The PROPER way to request a route is to 13.____

A. press the button corresponding to the desired route
B. press the button a number of times to correspond with the number of the route requested
C. stop at the signal and blow four short blasts
D. stop at the signal and telephone the tower

14. The motorman will know that his requested route has been registered in the tower if 14.____

A. a light comes on over the route request buttons
B. an acknowledging signal is sounded on the tower horn
C. the light in the route request button goes dark
D. the home signal continues to indicate stop

15. Under certain conditions, when stopped at such home signal, the motorman must signal for a signal maintainer and call the desk trainmaster. 15.____
Such condition exists when, after standing awhile,

A. the towerman continues to give the wrong route
B. the towerman does not acknowledge the signal
C. no route or call-on is given
D. the light over the route request buttons is cancelled out

16. It is clear that route request buttons 16.____

A. eliminate train delays due to signals at junctions
B. keep the towerman alert
C. force motormen and towermen to be more careful
D. are a more accurate form of communication than the whistle.

Questions 17-22.

DIRECTIONS: Questions 17 through 22 are to be answered on the basis of the instructions for removal of paper given below. Read these instructions carefully before answering these questions.

GENERAL INSTRUCTIONS FOR REMOVAL OF PAPER

When a cleaner's work schedule calls for the bagging of paper, he will remove paper from the waste paper receptacles, bag it, and place the bags at the head end of the platform, where they will be picked up by the work train. He will fill bags with paper to a weight that can be carried without danger of personal injury, as porters are forbidden to drag bags of paper over the platform. Cleaners are responsible that all bags of paper are arranged so as to prevent their falling from the platform to tracks, and so as to not interfere with passenger traffic.

17. A GOOD reason for removing the paper from receptacles and placing it in bags is that bags are more easily 17.____

A. stored B. weighed C. handled D. emptied

18. The *head end* of a local station platform is the end 18.____

    A. in the direction that trains are running
    B. nearest to which the trains stop
    C. where there is an underpass to the other side
    D. at which the change booth is located

19. The MOST likely reason for having the filled bags placed at the head end of the station rather than at the other end is that 19.____

    A. a special storage space is provided there for them
    B. this end of the platform is farthest from the passengers
    C. most porters' closets are located near the head end
    D. the work train stops at this end to pick them up

20. Limiting the weight to which the bags can be filled is PROBABLY done to 20.____

    A. avoid having too many ripped or broken bags
    B. protect the porter against possible rupture
    C. make sure that all bags are filled fairly evenly
    D. insure that, when stored, the bags will not fall to the track

21. The MOST important reason for not allowing filled bags to be dragged over the platform is that the bags 21.____

    A. could otherwise be loaded too heavily
    B. might leave streaks on the platform
    C. would wear out too quickly
    D. might spill paper on the platform

22. The instructions do NOT hold a porter responsible for a bag of paper which 22.____

    A. is torn due to dragging over a platform
    B. falls on a passenger because it was poorly stacked
    C. falls to the track without being pushed
    D. is ripped open by school children

Questions 23-25.

DIRECTIONS: Questions 23 through 25 are to be answered on the basis of the situation described below. Consider the facts given in this situation when answering these questions.

<u>SITUATION</u>

A new detergent that is to be added to water and the resulting mixture just wiped on any surface has been tested by the station department and appeared to be excellent. However, you notice, after inspecting a large number of stations that your porters have cleaned with this detergent, that the surfaces cleaned are not as clean as they formerly were when the old method was used.

23. The MAIN reason for the station department testing the new detergent in the first place was to make certain that 23.____

A. it was very simple to use
B. a little bit would go a long way
C. there was no stronger detergent on the market
D. it was superior to anything formerly used

24. The MAIN reason that such a poor cleaning job resulted was MOST likely due to the 24.____

A. porters being lax on the job
B. detergent not being as good as expected
C. incorrect amount of water being mixed with the detergent
D. fact that the surfaces cleaned needed to be scrubbed

25. The reason for inspecting a number of stations was to 25.____

A. determine whether all porters did the same job
B. insure that the result of the cleaning job was the same in each location
C. be certain that the detergent was used in each station inspected
D. see whether certain surfaces cleaned better than others

KEY (CORRECT ANSWERS)

1. A
2. C
3. D
4. A
5. C
6. B
7. C
8. B
9. C
10. D
11. C
12. C
13. A
14. A
15. C
16. D
17. C
18. A
19. D
20. B
21. C
22. D
23. D
24. B
25. B

PROBLEM SENSITIVITY

This section of the exam measures your ability to choose the course of action that should be taken first in critical situations.

Sample Questions

1. What should an officer do first when investigating an incident? 1.____

   A. Write a report of the incident.
   B. Inform other police officers of the incident.
   C. Proceed to the scene of the incident.
   D. Interview witnesses.

Getting the correct information to the emergency medical personnel is extremely important. It is suggested that you, the police officer, make the call if possible, or assign the task to a person who appears calm. If you are alone at the accident scene, do not leave the victim until breathing is restored, all bleeding has been stopped, the victim is no longer in danger of further injury, and all precautions have been taken against shock. When the emergency medical personnel arrive, brief them as to what happened to the victim, the type of first aid you have administered, and the physical status of the victim.

2. When the emergency medical personnel arrives at the accident scene, you first should tell them: 2.____

   A. how long the victim's breathing has been restored.
   B. how long the bleeding has been stopped.
   C. that the victim appeared to be going into shock.
   D. the type of first aid you administered.

KEY (CORRECT ANSWERS)

1. C
2. D

LOGICAL REASONING

INTRODUCTION

The ability to identify and resolve problems, and also to apply the principles of logic to given situations, is needed to perform many state jobs. These types of questions are designed to measure the applicant's ability in these areas.

1. If New York time is three hours ahead of San Francisco time, what time would it be in New York if a San Francisco clock one hour behind the time shows 4 o'clock? 1.____
   A. 1 o'clock B. 6 o'clock C. 7 o'clock D. 8 o'clock

2. Most of the Gaspard family lives in South Louisiana. Many of the people in South Louisiana celebrate Mardi Gras. Frank is a member of the Gaspard family. Based on these facts, we can conclude that 2.____
   A. Frank lives in South Louisiana.
   B. Frank does not celebrate Mardi Gras.
   C. All of the Gaspards celebrate Mardi Gras.
   D. None of the above can be concluded.

3. Bill must use Highway 19 to get to work. Bill has a meeting today at 9:00 A.M. If Bill misses the meeting, he probably will lose a major account. Highway 19 is closed all day due to repairs. Based on the above, we can conclude that: 3.____
   A. Bill will not be able to get to work.
   B. Bill will probably not be able to reschedule the meeting.
   C. Bill will lose a major account.
   D. None of the above can be concluded.

4. Mrs. Sellers reports that she was in the elevator late yesterday evening after leaving her office on the 15th floor of a large office building. A man got on at the 12th floor, pulled her off the elevator, an assaulted her, stealing her purse. She believes that she has seen the man in elevators and hallways of the building before. She thinks that he works in the building. 4.____
   Study the following parts of Mrs. Sellers' description of the man. Which one would be MOST useful in finding him, assuming that he is a regular occupant of the building?
   A. He had very bad breath.
   B. He was wearing a striped tie.
   C. He had a scar on his left cheek.
   D. He was carrying a blue backpack.

KEY (CORRECT ANSWERS)

1. The correct answer is D. If a San Francisco clock shows 4:00 and is one hour behind (slow), the actual time in San Francisco is 5:00. Therefore, the time in New York, which is three hours ahead, would be 8:00.

2. The correct answer is D. Choice A cannot be concluded, since most but not all of the Gaspard family lives in South Louisiana. Choice B is not supported by the passage at all. Choice C cannot be concluded, because the passage states that many, not all, people in South Louisiana celebrate Mardi Gras. Therefore, the answer is none of the above.

3. The correct answer is A. The passage does not address whether or not Bill will be able to reschedule his meeting, so choice B cannot be concluded. Choice C cannot be concluded, because the passage says he will probably lose a major account, but this is not a certainty. Choice A is a correct conclusion, because the passage states that Bill must use Highway 19 to get to work, and that Highway 19 is closed all day. Therefore, it can be concluded that Bill would not be able to get to work that day.

4. The correct answer is C. Choices A, B, and D all describe characteristics that could be easily changed or hidden. However, a scar on the face is noticeable and could not be easily disguised or removed. Therefore, the best answer is C.

EXAMINATION SECTION
TEST 1

DIRECTIONS: Below are 10 groups of statements and conclusions, numbered 1 through 10. For each group of statements, select the one conclusion lettered A, B, C, which is fully supported by and is based SOLELY on the statements. *PRINT THE LETTER OF THE CORRECT ANSWER IN THE SPACE AT THE RIGHT.*

1. He is either approved or disapproved for this examination. But, he is not approved. Therefore, he is 1.____

   A. qualified B. disapproved C. a taxpayer

2. In planning the itinerary for Mr. Kane, his secretary told him: Route 20 runs parallel to Route 6. Route 6 runs parallel to Route 18. 2.____
   Mr. Kane concluded that,
   Therefore, Route

   A. 20 is north of Route 6
   B. 18 intersects Route 20
   C. 20 is parallel to Route 18

3. Either the valedictorian is more intelligent than the salutatorian, or as intelligent, or less intelligent. 3.____
   But the valedictorian is not more intelligent, nor is she less intelligent.
   Therefore, the valedictorian is

   A. less intelligent than the salutatorian
   B. as intelligent as the salutatorian
   C. more intelligent than the salutatorian

4. If the date for the examination is changed, it will be held July 28, or it will be postponed until October 15. 4.____
   The date is not changed.
   Therefore, the examination

   A. will probably be held July 28
   B. date is uncertain
   C. will be held July 28, or it will be postponed until October 15

5. Joan transcribes faster than Nancy. 5.____
   Nancy transcribes faster than Anne.
   Therefore,

   A. Nancy transcribes faster than Joan
   B. Joan transcribes faster than Anne
   C. Nancy has had longer experience than Anne in taking dictation

6. The files in Division D contain either pending matter, completed case records, or dead material. 6.____
   They do not contain pending matter.
   Therefore, they contain

A. completed case records
B. completed case records and dead material
C. either completed case records or dead material

7. Either stenographer B in pool C types faster than stenographer A in pool D, or she types at the same rate as stenographer A, or she types slower than stenographer A. But, she does not type faster than stenographer A, nor does she type slower than stenographer Therefore, stenographer 7.____

A. B does not type as fast as stenographer A
B. B is more efficient than stenographer A
C. A types as fast as stenographer B

8. Miss Andre can be eligible for retirement when she has been in city service 35 years, or if she is 55 years of age. She is fifty-four years old and has been in city service 36 years. Therefore, she 8.____

A. is not eligible for retirement now
B. is eligible for retirement now
C. will be eligible for retirement only if she stays in city service for another year

9. If K is L, O is P; if M is N, Q is R.
Either K is L, or M is N.
Therefore, 9.____

A. K is P or M is R
B. either O is P or Q is R
C. the conclusion is uncertain

10. If the employee is in error, the supervisor's refusal to listen to his side is unreasonable. If he is not in error, the supervisor's refusal is unjust. But the employee is in error or he is not.
Therefore, the supervisor's refusal 10.____

A. may be considered later
B. is either unreasonable or it is unjust
C. is justifiable

KEY (CORRECT ANSWERS)

1. B	6. C
2. C	7. C
3. B	8. B
4. B	9. B
5. B	10. B

TEST 2

Questions 1-5

DIRECTIONS: Below are 5 groups of statements and conclusions, numbered 1 through 5. For each group of statements, select the one conclusion lettered A, B, C, which is fully supported by and is based SOLELY on the statements. *PRINT THE LETTER OF THE CORRECT ANSWER IN THE SPACE AT THE RIGHT.*

1. Three desks are placed in a straight row just inside the door in our office. Desk 1 is farther from the door than Desk 2. Desk 3 is farther from the door than Desk 1. Which desk is in the middle position from the door? Desk 1.____

   A. 1 B. 2 C. 3

2. The problem is either correct or incorrect or is unsolvable. 2.____
   The problem is not correct.
   Therefore, the

   A. problem is incorrect
   B. problem is either incorrect or is unsolvable
   C. conclusion is uncertain

3. Village E is situated between City F and Village G. 3.____
   City F is situated between Village G and Town H.
   Therefore, Village E is

   A. not situated between Village G and Town H
   B. situated between City F and Town H
   C. situated nearer to City F than to Town H

4. Jurisdiction No. 1 is between Jurisdictions No. 2 and No. 3. 4.____
   Jurisdiction No. 2 is between Jurisdictions No. 3 and No. 4.
   Therefore, Jurisdiction No. 1 is

   A. not between Jurisdictions No. 3 and No. 4
   B. between Jurisdictions No. 2 and No. 4
   C. nearer to Jurisdiction No. 2 than to No. 4

5. Five candidates (A, B, C, D, and E) are seated in the same room. D is between A and B, E is between A and D: C is the same distance from A and E, and D is the same distance from A and B. 5.____
   Therefore,

   A. E is nearer to B than to A
   B. C is nearer to E than to D
   C. B is nearer to E than to D

Questions 6-10.

DIRECTIONS: Each question or incomplete statement is followed by several suggested answers or completions. Select the one that BEST answers the question or completes the statement. *PRINT THE LETTER OF THE CORRECT ANSWER IN THE SPACE AT THE RIGHT.*

6. If John is older than Mary and Mary is younger than Jane, then 6.____

A. twice Mary's age is less than the sum of the ages of John and Jane
B. the sum of the ages of John and Mary exceeds the age of Jane
C. the ages of John and Jane are equal
D. three times Mary's age equals the sum of the ages of John and Jane

7. John is older than Mary, Henry is older than Mary. 7.____
It follows, therefore, that

A. John and Henry are the same age
B. the sum of the ages of John and Mary exceeds the age of Henry
C. Mary's age is less than half of the sum of John's and Henry's ages
D. none of the preceding three statements is true

8. The average of 9 numbers is 70. 8.____
It follows that

A. the sum of the numbers is 630
B. the median of the numbers is 70
C. the median of the numbers cannot be 70
D. no two of the numbers can be equal

9. John is twice as old as Mary. 9.____
The only statement about their ages which is NOT true is

A. in five years, John will be twice as old as Mary
B. in five years, the sum of their ages will be 10 more than the present sum of their ages
C. Mary's present age is one-third of the sum of their present ages
D. two years ago, the difference between their ages was the same as it will be two years hence

10. A is taller than B; C is 2 inches shorter than B. 10.____
The one statement of the following four statements which is NOT necessarily true is

A. B is taller than C
B. A is taller than C
C. A is taller than C by more than 2 inches
D. B's height is the average of the heights of A and C

KEY (CORRECT ANSWERS)

1. A	6. A
2. B	7. C
3. C	8. D
4. C	9. A
5. B	10. D

TEST 3

DIRECTIONS: Each question or incomplete statement is followed by several suggested answers or completions. Select the one that BEST answers the question or completes the statement. *PRINT THE LETTER OF THE CORRECT ANSWER IN THE SPACE AT THE RIGHT.*

1. A stenographer can BEST deal with the situation which arises when her pencil breaks during dictation by 1.____

   A. asking the person dictating to lend her one
   B. being equipped at every dictation with several pencils
   C. going back to her desk to secure another one
   D. making a call to the supply room for some pencils

2. Accuracy is of greater importance than speed in filing CHIEFLY because 2.____

   A. city offices have a tremendous amount of filing to do
   B. fast workers are usually inferior workers
   C. there is considerable difficulty in locating materials which have been filed incorrectly
   D. there are many varieties of filing systems which may be used

3. Many persons dictate so rapidly that they pay little attention to matters of punctuation and English, but they expect their stenographers to correct errors. 3.____
   This statement implies MOST clearly that stenographers should be

   A. able to write acceptable original reports when required
   B. good citizens as well as good stenographers
   C. efficient clerks as well as good stenographers
   D. efficient in language usage

4. A typed letter should resemble a picture properly framed. 4.____
   This statement MOST emphasizes

   A. accuracy B. speed
   C. convenience D. neatness

5. Of the following, the CHIEF advantage of the use of a mechanical check is that it 5.____

   A. guards against tearing in handling the check
   B. decreases the possibility of alteration in the amount of the check
   C. tends to prevent the mislaying and loss of checks
   D. facilitates keeping checks in proper order for mailing

6. Of the following, the CHIEF advantage of the use of a dictating machine is that the 6.____

   A. stenographer must be able to take rapid dictation
   B. person dictating tends to make few errors
   C. dictator may be dictating letters while the stenographer is busy at some other task
   D. usual noise in an office is lessened

7. The CHIEF value of indicating enclosures beneath the identification marks on the lower left side of a letter is that it 7.____

A. acts as a check upon the contents before mailing and upon receiving a letter
B. helps determine the weight for mailing
C. is useful in checking the accuracy of typed matter
D. requires an efficient mailing clerk

8. The one of the following which is NOT an advantage of the window envelope is that it 8.____

A. saves time since the inside address serves also as an outside address
B. gives protection to the address from wear and tear of the mails
C. lessens the possibility of mistakes since the address is written only once
D. tends to be much easier to seal than the plain envelope

9. A question as to proper syllabication of a word at the end of a line may BEST be settled by consulting 9.____

A. the person who dictated the letter
B. a shorthand manual
C. a dictionary
D. a file of letters

10. Mailing a letter which contains many erasures is undesirable CHIEFLY because 10.____

A. paper should not be wasted
B. some stenographers are able to carry on some of the correspondence in an office without consulting their superiors
C. correspondence should be neat
D. erasures indicate that the dictator was not certain of what he intended to say in the letter

---

KEY (CORRECT ANSWERS)

1. B	6. C
2. C	7. A
3. D	8. D
4. D	9. C
5. B	10. C

TEST 4

DIRECTIONS: Each question or incomplete statement is followed by several suggested answers or completions. Select the one that BEST answers the question or completes the statement. *PRINT THE LETTER OF THE CORRECT ANSWER IN THE SPACE AT THE RIGHT.*

1. A charter operates for a city in somewhat the same fashion as 1.____

   A. the United States Supreme Court functions with regard to federal legislation
   B. the United States Constitution operates for the entire country
   C. the Governor functions for New York State
   D. a lease for a landlord

2. All civil employees should be especially interested in the activities of the United States Supreme Court PRIMARILY because 2.____

   A. its decisions provide certain kinds of important general rules
   B. the Supreme Court consists of nine persons appointed by the President
   C. the American Constitution is the finest document which man has ever produced
   D. the President's plan for reorganization of the court may be revived

3. Of the following, it is most frequently argued that labor problems are of concern to the civil employee PRIMARILY because 3.____

   A. the problems of labor are the same as the problems of government
   B. newspapers carry considerable information about labor problems
   C. the civil employee is a wage or salary earner
   D. a government is of the people, for the people, and by the people

4. Warfare in any part of the world should be of interest to the civil employee PRIMARILY as a result of the fact that 4.____

   A. strict American neutrality is secured by not permitting the sale of munitions to any country at war
   B. war has not been declared though warfare is raging
   C. the United States participates in the meetings of the UN
   D. facilities for transportation and communication have produced a "smaller" world

5. Cities regulate certain aspects of housing CHIEFLY because 5.____

   A. the city is the largest municipality in the country
   B. zoning is the concern of all residents of the city
   C. housing affects health
   D. the state constitution makes regulation optional

6. In general, it is PROBABLY true that the functions which a city administers are those 6.____

   A. most necessary to the preservation of the well-being of its residents
   B. of little or no interest to private business
   C. forbidden to the state
   D. not capable of being financed by private business

7. There is no more convincing mark of a cultured speaker or writer than accuracy of statement. 7.____
This statement stresses the importance of

   A. new ideas
   B. facts
   C. acquiring a pleasing speaking voice
   D. poise

8. When a department is called, the voice which answers the telephone is, to the person calling, the department itself. 8.____
This statement implies *most clearly* that

   A. only one person should answer the telephone in each office
   B. a clerk with a pleasing, courteous telephone manner is an asset to an office
   C. an efficient clerk will terminate all telephone conversations as quickly as possible
   D. making personal telephone calls is looked upon with disfavor in some offices

9. Probably the CHIEF advantage of filling higher vacancies by promotion is that this procedure 9.____

   A. stimulates the worker to improve his work and general knowledge and technique
   B. provides an easy check on the work of the individual
   C. eliminates personnel problems in a department
   D. harmonizes the work of one department with that of all other departments

10. Greatest efficiency is reached when filing method and filing clerk are harmoniously adjusted to the needs of an office. 10.____
This statement means *most nearly* that

   A. the filing method is more important than the clerk in securing the successful handling of valuable papers
   B. almost any clerk can do office filing well
   C. a good clerk using a good filing system assures good filing
   D. every office needs a filing system

KEY (CORRECT ANSWERS)

1.	B	6.	A
2.	A	7.	B
3.	C	8.	B
4.	D	9.	A
5.	C	10.	C

TEST 5

DIRECTIONS: Each question or incomplete statement is followed by several suggested answers or completions. Select the one that BEST answers the question or completes the statement. *PRINT THE LETTER OF THE CORRECT ANSWER IN THE SPACE AT THE RIGHT.*

1. Your superior, Mr. Hotchkiss, is in conference and has requested that he not be disturbed. 1.____
The condition under which you would MOST probably disturb the conference is:

    A. A Mr. Smith, whom you have not seen before, says he has important business with Mr, Hotchkiss
    B. Mrs. Hotchkiss telephones, saying there has been a serious accident at home
    C. You do not know how a certain letter should be filed and wish to ask the advice of Mr. Hotchkiss
    D. A fellow clerk wishes to ask Mr. Hotchkiss whether a particular city department handles certain matters

2. Your superior directs you to find certain papers. You know the purpose for which the papers are to be used. In the course of your search for the papers, you come across certain material which would be very useful for the purpose to be served by the papers. 2.____
You should

    A. bring the papers to your superior and ask whether he wants the other materials
    B. go to your superior immediately and ask whether he wishes both the materials and the papers or only one of the two
    C. bring to your superior the other materials, together with the papers you were directed to find
    D. bring only the other materials to your superior and point out the manner in which these materials are of greater value than the papers

3. If a fellow employee asks you a question to which you do not know the answer, you should say, 3.____

    A. "I don't know. What's the difference?"
    B. "The answer to that question forms no part of my duties here."
    C. "My dear sir, the thing for you to do is to look the matter up yourself because it is your responsibility, not mine."
    D. "I'm sorry. I don't know."

4. In general, it is PROBABLY true that MOST people are 4.____

    A. so self-seeking that they pay no attention to the wants, needs, or behavior of others
    B. so changeable that one never knows what his fellow employee is likely to do next
    C. not worth the trouble to bother about
    D. quite ready to help others

5. Of the following, the one which is NOT a reason for avoiding clerical errors is that 5.____

    A. time is lost
    B. money is wasted
    C. many clerks are very intelligent
    D. serious consequences may follow

6. Of the following, the MAIN reason for keeping a careful record of incoming mail is that 6.____

   A. some people are less industrious than others
   B. this record helps to speed up outgoing mail
   C. this record is a kind of legal evidence
   D. this information may be useful in answering questions which may arise

7. Of the following, the MAIN reason for using a calculating machine is that 7.____

   A. a lesser knowledge of arithmetic is needed
   B. a more attractive product is obtained
   C. greater speed and accuracy are obtained
   D. it is not difficult to learn how to operate a calculating machine

8. Of the following, the MAIN reason for being polite over the telephone is that 8.____

   A. persons who are speaking over the telephone cannot see each other
   B. politeness makes for pleasant business relationships
   C. it is not at all difficult or costly to be courteous
   D. one's voice is of great importance because voice reflects mood

9. Because telephone directories contain printed pages, they are called books. This statement assumes *most nearly* that 9.____

   A. some books do not contain printed pages
   B. not all telephone directories are books which contain printed pages
   C. material which contains printed pages is called a book
   D. all books which contain printed pages are called telephone directories

10. Mr. Cross must be using a budget because he has been able to reduce his unnecessary expenses. 10.____
    On the basis of only the material included in this statement, it may MOST accurately be said that this statement assumes that

    A. all people who use budgets lower certain types of expenses
    B. some people who do not use budgets reduce unnecessary expenses
    C. some people who use budgets do not reduce unnecessary expenses
    D. all types of expenses are reduced by the use of a budget

---

KEY (CORRECT ANSWERS)

1. B	6. D
2. C	7. C
3. D	8. B
4. D	9. C
5. C	10. A

EXAMINATION SECTION
TEST 1

DIRECTIONS: Each question or incomplete statement is followed by several suggested answers or completions. Select the one that BEST answers the question or completes the statement. *PRINT THE LETTER OF THE CORRECT ANSWER IN THE SPACE AT THE RIGHT.*

QUESTIONS 1-4.

Questions 1-4 refer to the following information.

A recent study shows that of the 1000 graduates of Learnmore High School, 40% claimed that they smoked during their high school years, 30% said they started smoking before entering high school and continued smoking during high school years. Of the people who didn't smoke at all during their high school year, 70% claim that they have no medical problems. However, only 10% of those who did smoke during their high school years reported no medical problem.

1. What percent of all these graduates claim they have NO medical problem? 1.____

   A. 30
   B. 42
   C. 60
   D. 70
   E. None of the above

2. How many non-smokers have had at LEAST one medical problem? 2.____

   A. 70 B. 180 C. 280 D. 350 E. 450

3. What is the MAXIMUM number of people who began smoking before entering high school, and have had NO medical problems? 3.____

   A. 10 B. 30 C. 40 D. 100 E. over 100

4. Counting only individuals who have experienced at least one medical problem, what is the ratio of those who didn't smoke during high school years to those who did smoke during that time period? 4.____

   A. 3:2 B. 1:2 C. 1:3 D. 2:3 E. 3:1

5. If John enjoys the taste of pineapple, he'll like the taste of all fruit. The preceding statement is MOST similar to which of the following? 5.____

   A. If a dog has a liking for human food, he'll like all dog food
   B. If a person can understand algebra, he can understand all mathematics
   C. If a Chevrolet gets good gas mileage, then so will a Datsun
   D. If Sue's favorite color is red, then she won't buy a green dress
   E. If Bob can fix any electrical item, then he can fix a toaster

6. Only a few people who are heavy smokers will live past the age of 90. Since Eve is a 30-year-old non-smoker, she will probably live beyond the age of 90. 6.____
   The argument is MOST similar to which of the following?

A. Only a few cities like Cleanville have a low crime rate. Thus, if a person lives in a low crime rate city, that city must be Cleanville.
B. Only birds have feathers. Thus, some birds have morefeathers than other birds.
C. All weight-lifters are light sleepers. Since Bob is a heavy sleeper, he doesn't lift weights.
D. Not many individuals who worry a lot can get a good night's rest. Since John does not worry at all, he can probably get a good night's rest.
E. Some mathematicians enjoy all sports. Since William is a mathematician, he may not enjoy any sports.

7. Since Jack is left-handed, he is an excellent tennis player. Assuming that the preceding statement is true, from which one(s) of the following can this quoted statement be logically deduced? 7.____

I. All tennis players are left-handed.
II. None of the excellent tennis players is right-handed.
III. Either Jack is right-handed or he is an excellent tennis player.

A. I only B. II only C. III only
D. II and III E. I, II, and III

8. Gamblers are boisterous individuals. Yesterday, I went to the racetrack and there was a lot of shouting after every race. The above argument assumes: 8.____

I. Gamblers frequent racetracks.
II. Noisy people are gamblers.
III. Quiet people don't go to racetracks.

A. I only B. II only C. III only
D. I, III E. I, II, III

QUESTIONS 9-14.

Questions 9-14 refer to the facts below. It is to be assumed that it is the month of July, the first day of which is a Monday.

The All-Weather appliance store sells televisions, radios, toasters, and refrigerators. Certain conditions govern this store:

I. The store is open only Monday through Friday every month. Thus, all purchases and deliveries can only be made Monday through Friday.
II. TV's and radios are only delivered on even numbered days.
III. Refrigerators are delivered only on Tuesdays and Thursdays.
IV. Toasters are delivered on any date of the month which can be divided evenly by 3 or 5.
V. A customer may purchase a radio or a toaster on the day of delivery.
VI. Since refrigerators and TV's are more expensive items, they are immediately inspected on the day of delivery. However, a customer may not purchase these items until 3 business days after delivery.

9. Which item(s) could be neither delivered nor purchased on Wednesdays? 9.____

A. TV's and radios B. TV's, radios, and refrigerators
C. Refrigerators and toasters D. Refrigerators *only*
E. Toasters *only*

10. On how many days during this month can toasters be purchased? 10.____

A. At least 4 but fewer than 7
B. 9
C. 11
D. More than 11
E. None of the above

11. During the first week, on which dates may a TV either be purchased or delivered? 11.____

A. 2nd, 3rd, 4th
B. 2nd, 4th, 5th
C. 3rd, 4th, 5th
D. 2nd, 5th, 6th
E. 2nd, 3rd

12. On how many days during this month can TV's be delivered? 12.____

A. Fewer than 6
B. 8
C. 9
D. 10
E. 11

13. What is the *earliest* date on which both a TV and toaster can be purchased? 13.____

A. 3rd
B. 5th
C. 7th
D. 9th
E. 11th

14. Which appliance(s) has(have) exactly 2 delivery dates on Fridays? 14.____

A. Toasters, radios, TV's
B. Toasters, TV's
C. TV's, radios
D. Toasters, radios
E. Only toasters

15. If a person studies hard, he can pass any high school course. 15.____
This statement can be logically deduced from which of the following?

A. Some people study while others don't study.
B. A person who has passed a particular high school course must have studied hard.
C. A high school course can be passed if a person is willing to study hard.
D. If a person doesn't study, he can't expect to pass a high school course.
E. Some high school courses require more studying than do other courses.

QUESTIONS 16-17.

Questions 16 and 17 are to be answered on the basis of the following.

The most dangerous sport in the world is thoroughbred horseracing, since more participants per thousand are killed than in any other sport. Hang-gliding is the second most dangerous sport. By contrast, boxing ranks tenth on the list of most dangerous sports.

16. The author of the above paragraph is *most likely* trying to convey the message that: 16.____

A. Most sports are dangerous
B. Hang-gliding is popular despite its danger
C. Only ten sports are considered dangerous
D. The most number of injuries occur in horseracing
E. Boxing is not the most dangerous sport

17. The author would *probably* be opposed to: 17.____

A. Any dangerous sport
B. A ban on boxing
C. Amateur boxing
D. Horseracing
E. A ban on horseracing

QUESTIONS 18-22.

Questions 18-22 are to be answered on the basis of the following.
The Expanding Food Company has outlet stores on each of First Ave., Second Ave., Third Ave., Fourth Ave., and Fifth Ave. Also, it is known that:

I. There is at least one store on each avenue.
II. The number of stores on Fifth Ave. equals the sum of the number of stores on First Ave. plus those on Second Ave.
III. The number of stores on Second Ave. is double the number of stores on Third Ave.
IV. The number of stores on Fourth Ave. is greater than the number of stores on Fifth Ave.
V. There are an even number of stores on First Ave.

18. What is the *fewest* number of stores that must exist on Fourth Ave.? 18.____

A. 2 B. 3 C. 4 D. 5 E. 6

19. Which avenue has the MOST stores? 19.____

A. Fifth Ave. B. Fourth Ave.
C. Third Ave. D. All of the above
E. None of the above

20. Suppose NO avenue has *more* than 7 stores. Find the total number of stores on all 5 avenues. 20.____

A. 16 or 19 B. 20
C. 21 D. 16, 19 or 20
E. 16, 20 or 21

21. The number of stores on Fifth Ave 21.____

A. must be even
B. must be odd
C. could equal the number of stores on First Ave.
D. could equal the number of stores on Second Ave.
E. none of the above

22. Suppose it is known that there are 4 stores on Third Ave. and that there are *more* than 4 stores on First Ave. 22.____
Find the *minimum* number of stores on all 5 avenues.

A. 45 B. 49 C. 46 D. 48 E. 47

QUESTIONS 23-25.

Questions 23 through 25 are to be answered on the basis Gf the following.

In a particular group of 21 people, each individual is one of three professions: doctor, engineer, or teacher. Half the number of people who smoke are engineers. One-third of the number of non-smokers are doctors. The number of engineers who smoke equals the number of non-smokers who are not doctors.

23. How many of the non-smokers are doctors? 23.____

A. 2 B. 3 C. 5 D. 6 E. 9

24. If all the teachers are smokers, and there are only 2 doctors who smoke, then the teachers represent ______ Percent of the entire group. 24.____

A. 19 B. 25 C. 29 D. 33 E. 40

25. Using the information from the preceding question, *how many* engineers are there in the entire group? 25.____

A. 3 B. 6 C. 9 D. 12 E. 15

KEY (CORRECT ANSWERS)

1. E
2. B
3. C
4. B
5. B
6. D
7. C
8. A
9. D
10. E
11. B
12. E
13. B
14. A
15. C
16. E
17. B
18. D
19. B
20. E
21. A
22. E
23. B
24. A
25. D

SOLUTIONS

1. (.70)(.60) = .42 of all the graduates didn't smoke and didn't have any medical problems, whereas (.10)(.40) = .04 of all the graduates did smoke but yet didn't experience any medical problems. Thus, .42 + .04 = .46 or 46% of all graduates claimed they had no medical problems.

(ANSWER E).

2. (.30)(.60) = .18 of the population were non-smokers and yet had at least one medical problem. Now (.18)(1000) = 180.

(ANSWER B).

3. (.10)(.40) = .04 indicates the number of people who did smoke during their high school years and had no medical problem. Of the .04, it is not possible to determine what fraction actually started smoking before entering high school. So, (.04)(1000) = 40.

(ANSWER C).

4. (.30)(.60) = .18 of the non-smokers had at least one medical problem, whereas (.90)(.40) = .36 of the smokers had at least one medical problem. Then .18/.36 = 1:2 ratio.

(ANSWER B).

5. The original statement uses the truth of a specific item in order to imply the truth of a general item containing that specific item. Only choice B illustrates that kind of reasoning.

(ANSWER B).

6. The original statement can be written: "If A, then B. If not A, then not B." This argument is not necessarily valid, but choice D resembles it most closely.

(ANSWER D).

7. Statement I is false, since we can assume that there exist both left-handed and right-handed players. Statement II is also false, because there may be excellent right-handed players. Statement III is true, since Jack is not right-handed and thus would have to be an excellent tennis player.

(ANSWER C).

8. The only valid implication is Statement I, since one can assume that gamblers do visit racetracks. (This statement could be false, since it is only an assumption). Statement II is not valid since many types of people are noisy. Statement III is also invalid since one can assume that both noisy and quiet people frequent racetracks.

(ANSWER A).

QUESTIONS 9-14.

Questions 9-14 see calendars below showing days of receiving and purchasing of each of the 4 different appliances. Note that for question #10, the actual answer is 10.

7 (#1)

Radio Delivered / TV Delivered

Sun	Mon	Tu	Wed	Th	Fri	Sat
	1	**2**	3	**4**	5	6
7	**8**	9	**10**	11	**12**	13
14	15	**16**	17	**18**	19	20
21	**22**	23	**24**	25	**26**	27
28	29	**30**	31			

Toaster Delivered

Sun	Mon	Tu	Wed	Th	Fri	Sat
	1	2	**3**	4	**5**	6
7	8	**9**	**10**	11	**12**	13
14	**15**	16	17	**18**	19	20
21	22	23	**24**	**25**	26	27
28	29	**30**	31			

Refrigerator Delivered

Sun	Mon	Tu	Wed	Th	Fri	Sat
	1	**2**	3	**4**	5	6
7	8	**9**	10	**11**	12	13
14	15	**16**	17	**18**	19	20
21	22	**23**	24	**25**	26	27
28	29	**30**	31			

Radio Purchased

Sun	Mon	Tu	Wed	Th	Fri	Sat
	1	**2**	3	**4**	5	6
7	**8**	9	**10**	11	**12**	13
14	15	**16**	17	**18**	19	20
21	**22**	23	**24**	25	**26**	27
28	29	**30**	31			

8 (#1)

Radio Purchased

Sun	Mon	Tu	Wed	Th	Fri	Sat
	1	②	3	④	5	6
7	⑧	9	⑩	11	⑫	13
14	15	⑯	17	⑱	19	20
21	㉒	23	㉔	25	㉖	27
28	29	㉚	31			

Toaster Purchased

Sun	Mon	Tu	Wed	Th	Fri	Sat
	1	2	③	4	⑤	6
7	8	⑨	⑩	11	⑫	13
14	⑮	16	17	⑱	19	20
21	22	23	㉔	㉕	26	27
28	29	㉚	31			

TV Purchased

Sun	Mon	Tu	Wed	Th	Fri	Sat
	1	2	3	4	⑤	6
7	8	⑨	10	⑪	12	13
14	⑮	16	⑰	18		20
21	22	㉓	24	㉕	26	27
28	㉙	30	㉛			

Refrigerator Purchased

Sun	Mon	Tu	Wed	Th	Fri	Sat
	1	2	3	4	⑤	6
7	8	⑨	10	11	⑫	13
14	15	⑯	17	18	⑲	20
21	22	㉓	24	25	㉖	27
28	29	㉚	31			

9. (ANSWER D).
10. (ANSWER E).
11. (ANSWER B).
12. (ANSWER E).
13. (ANSWER B).

14. (ANSWER A).

15. The original statement follows logically from choice C, since it implies that studying hard is a prerequisite to passing any high school course.

(ANSWER C).

16. Although the general public perceives boxing as the most dangerous sport(or at least one of the most dangerous), the author is relying on a certain type of statistic to illustrate that there are nine other sports which could be considered more dangerous than boxing.

(ANSWER E).

17. The author, by his argument, appears to be defending any ban on the sport of boxing. He does not make any case for or against another sport.

(ANSWER B).

18. Let x, 2y, y, w, z be the number of stores respectively on First, Second, Third, Fourth, and Fifth Avenues. Also, $z = x + 2y$, $w > z$, and x must be an even number. Since the smallest values for x and y are 2 and 1 respectively, the minimum value of $z = 2 + (2)(1) = 4$. Now w = the number of stores on Fourth Ave., and since $w > z$, then $w > 4$. Thus, 5 is the minimum value of w.

(ANSWER D).

19. Since $z = x + 2y$, $z > x$ and $z > y$. But $w > z$, so that w is the variable with the highest value. We know that w = the number of stores on Fourth Ave.

(ANSWER B).

20. Assume $z = 7$. Then there are two e possible combinations of numbers associated with the number of stores on First, Second, Third, Fourth, and Fifth Avenues respectively. The 1st combination is 2, 4, 2, 7, 6; the 2nd combination is 4, 2, 1, 7, 6; the 3rd combination is 2, 2, 1, 7, 4. Thus, only 16, 20, or 21 are the possible totals.

(ANSWER E).

21. Since $z = x + 2y$ and x must be even, then z must also be an even number. Note that 2y is already even. Thus, even number + even number = even number.

(ANSWER A).

22. Since Third Ave. has 4 stores, Second Ave. has 8 stores. We also know that First Ave. has more than 4 stores; thus it must have a minimum of 6 stores (even number). Fifth Ave. has $6 + 8 = 14$ stores at minimum, and 15 = the minimum stores on Fourth Ave. Thus, the number of stores on all 5 avenues (minimum) $= 6 + 8 + 4 + 14 + 15 = 47$.

(ANSWER E).

23. Let x = # of smokers, so that 21 - x = # of non-smokers. Then 1/2x = # of smokers who are also engineers. This number must equal the number of non-smokers who are not doctors. We can infer that 2/3 of the non-smokers (i.e. 2/3 [21 - x]) are not doctors. Thus, $1/2x = 2/3\,(21 - x)$. So, $x = 12$ and $21 - x = 9$. This implies that there are a total of 9 non-smokers. Since 1/3 of this number are doctors, there are 3 non-smoking doctors.

(ANSWER B).

24. Since 1/2 of the smokers are engineers, this translates to (1/2)(12) = 6 people. Only 2 doctors smoke, so the number of teachers who smoke = 12 - 6 - 2 = 4. (All teachers are smokers). Now 4/21 = .1905 or approximately 19%.

(ANSWER A).

25. The non-smokers must consist of only doctors and engineers. Of the 9 non-smokers, 3 are doctors. Thus 6 non-smokers are engineers. We already know that there are 6 engineers who smoke, so that there are a total of 12 engineers.

(ANSWER D).

EXAMINATION SECTION
TEST 1

DIRECTIONS: Each question or incomplete statement is followed by several suggested answers or completions. Select the one that BEST answers the question or completes the statement. *PRINT THE LETTER OF THE CORRECT ANSWER IN THE SPACE AT THE RIGHT.*

Questions 1-4.

DIRECTIONS: Questions 1 through 4 are to be answered on the basis of the following passage.

A State department which is interested in finding acceptable solutions to the operational problems of specific types of community self-help organizations recently sent two of its staff members to meet with one such organization. At that meeting, the leaders of the community organization voiced the need for increased activity planning input of a more detailed nature from the citizens regularly served by that organization. There followed a discussion of a number of information-gathering methods, including surveys by telephone, questionnaires mailed to the citizens' residences, in-person interviews with the citizens, and the placing of suggestion boxes in the organization's headquarters building. Concern was expressed by one of the leaders that the organization's funds be spent judiciously. The State department representatives present promised to investigate the possibility of a matching fund grant of money to the organization.

Later, the proposed survey was conducted using questionnaires completed by those citizens who visited the organization's headquarters. The results of the survey included the information that twice as many citizens wanted more educational activities scheduled than wanted more social activities scheduled, whereas one-half of those who wanted more educational activities scheduled were interested mainly in special job training.

1. A similar survey conducted by a State department employee involved special job training. That survey uncovered the information below. The following four sentences are to be rearranged to form the most effective and logical paragraph. Select the letter representing the best sequence for these sentences. 1.____
    - I. The majority of those who are still in this group are ethnic minorities.
    - II. The number of economically disadvantaged people who enjoyed their special job training is larger than the number of economically disadvantaged people who did not enjoy it.
    - III. Thirty-five percent of all those who are economically disadvantaged are not ethnic minorities.
    - IV. Eighty percent of those who have completed special job training in the past ten years are economically disadvantaged.

    The CORRECT answer is:

    A. IV, I, III, II
    B. I, III, II, IV
    C. IV, II, I, III
    D. I, II, III, IV

2. In the reading passage above, the word *judiciously* means MOST NEARLY 2.____

    A. legally
    B. immediately
    C. prudently
    D. uniformly

3. Based *only* on the information in the reading passage, which one of the following statements is MOST fully supported? 3.____
   A. The leaders of the community organization in question wanted to increase the quantity and quality of feedback about that organization's suggestion boxes.
   B. The number of citizens surveyed who wanted more educational activities scheduled and were mainly interested in special job training was the same as the number of citizens surveyed who wanted more social activities to be scheduled.
   C. At the meeting concerned, matching funds were promised to the community organization in question by the two State department representatives present.
   D. Telephone surveys generally yield more accurate information than do surveys conducted through the use of mailed questionnaires.

4. The following four sentences are to be rearranged to form the most effective and logical paragraph. Select the letter representing the best sequence for these sentences. 4.____
   I. Formal surveys of citizens within a community also convey to those citizens the interest of the community leadership in hearing the citizens' ideas about community improvement.
   II. Such surveys can provide needed input into the process of establishing specific community program goals.
   III. Formally conducted surveys of community residents often yield valuable information to the local area leaders responsible for community-based programs.
   IV. No community should formulate these goals without attempting to obtain the views of its citizenry.

   The CORRECT answer is:

   A. III, I, IV, II
   B. I, III, II, IV
   C. III, II, IV, I
   D. IV, III, II, I

Questions 5-8.

DIRECTIONS: Questions 5 through 8 are to be answered on the basis of the following passage.

The Smith Paint Company, which currently employs 2,000 persons, has been in existence for 20 years. A new chemical paint, Futuron, was recently developed by an employee of that company. This paint was released for public use a month ago on a trial basis. The sales were phenomenal, and there is a great demand for more Futuron to be manufactured. The profits to be made by increased manufacturing and sale of Futuron could place the Smith Paint Company in a leading role in the paint industry.

The Smith Paint Company currently produces 2 million gallons of the more traditional paint per year. The Smith Paint Company's Board of Directors wishes to reduce its production of this traditional paint by 50%, and to produce 1 million gallons of Futuron per year.

The employees are quite concerned about this potential production change. A public nonprofit research group has been investigating the chemical make-up of Futuron. Initial research indicates that negative physical reactions may result from working closely with the chemicals necessary to manufacture Futuron. For this reason, most of the company employees do not want the proposed change in production to occur. The members of the Board of Directors, however, argue that the research results are too inconclusive to cause great concern. They say that the company would lose 25% to 50% of its potential profit if the large-scale manufacturing of Futuron is not initiated immediately.

5. Seventy-five percent of the Smith Paint Company's current employees were hired during its first 10 years of operation. Fifteen percent were hired in the past five years. During the five-year interval between the first ten years and the most recent five years, 40 persons were hired per year. 5._____
What percentage of its total employees were hired during the Smith Paint Company's first 13 years of operation?

A. 75% B. 81% C. 85% D. 90%

6. Assume that the total possible profit the Smith Paint Company could make during its first year of manufacturing the proposed amount of Futuron would be $1.00 per gallon. The purchase of new machinery would reduce this first-year profit by 50%. The anticipated delay, during the first production year, in establishing large-scale manufacturing facilities would reduce the total possible profit by an additional 25%. 6._____
Given this information, what would be the actual profit made from the first year of manufacturing Futuron?

A. $250,000 B. $375,000 C. $500,000 D. $750,000

7. In the reading passage, the word *inconclusive* means MOST NEARLY 7._____

A. ineluctable
B. incorrect
C. unreasonable
D. indeterminate

8. Based on the information in the reading passage, which of the following statements represents the MOST accurate conclusion? 8._____

A. The proposed reduction in the production of its traditional paint would not financially injure the Smith Paint Company.
B. A greater proportion of the Smith Paint Company's employees are in favor of the proposed increase in Futuron production than are opposed to it.
C. The increased Futuron production proposed by the Smith Paint Company's Board of Directors would cause that company's employees considerable health damage.
D. Positive public response to the sale of Futuron suggests that considerable profit can be made by increasing the manufacturing and sale of Futuron.

KEY (CORRECT ANSWERS)

1. A
2. C
3. B
4. C
5. B
6. A
7. D
8. D

SOLUTIONS TO PROBLEMS

1. For the following reasons, Choice A is correct and the other three choices are incorrect:

   1. Both Choice B and Choice D begin with Sentence I, which states, *The majority of those who are still in this group are ethnic minorities.* The paragraph cannot logically begin with a statement such as Sentence I, because no one reading the paragraph would know what *this group* refers to. Therefore, Choice B and Choice D are not correct and may be eliminated from consideration.

   2. Both Choice A and Choice C begin with Sentence IV, which states, *Eighty percent of those who have completed special job training in the past ten years are economically disadvantaged.* The problem then becomes selecting the best sequence of the other three sentences so that they most logically follow the initial Sentence IV.

   3. If you select Choice C, then you are choosing Sentence II as the correct second sentence. Sentence II states, *The number of economically disadvantaged people who enjoyed their special job training is larger than the number of economically disadvantaged people who did not enjoy it.* Then Sentence I would be the third sentence. However, that would not be logical, because you could not tell whether *this group* in Sentence I refers to *economically disadvantaged people who enjoyed their special job training* or whether *this group* refers to *economically disadvantaged people who did not enjoy it.* Therefore, Choice C is not correct.

   4. By the process of elimination, only Choice A remains. Choice A specifies Sentence I as the second sentence, which is logically correct in that *this group* in Sentence I will then refer to those who *are economically disadvantaged* in Sentence IV. The two remaining sentences also refer back to *economically disadvantaged,* thus creating a paragraph that reads logically from start to finish. Therefore, Choice A is the correct answer.

2. Choices B and D should be eliminated from further consideration due to the context in which the word *judiciously* was used in the reading passage. Specifically, concern was expressed that funds be spent judiciously. Nothing in the paragraph suggests a need for concern if the funds were not spent immediately or uniformly. Choice A must be considered, because public funds should be spent legally. However, the word *judiciously* is related to the word *judgment* rather than to the word *judiciary.* It is the latter word that has to do with courts of law and is related to legality, so Choice A is incorrect. On the other hand, *judiciously* and *prudently* both mean *wisely* and *with direction.* Therefore, Choice C is correct.

3. Choice B is the correct choice. No matter what numbers you apply, Choice B still will be correct. This is because when you multiply any number by two and then divide the result in half, you end up with the same number that you began with. For example, suppose that 20 citizens wanted more social activities. Twice that number (40 citizens) wanted more educational activities. But of those 40 citizens, one-half (20 citizens) wanted mainly special job training.

Choice A is incorrect because, first of all, the organization did not have any suggestion boxes; although suggestion boxes were discussed, questionnaires ultimately were used instead. In addition, Choice A is incorrect because it was input about the planning of activities that the leaders of the community organization wanted rather than feedback concerning suggestion boxes.

Choice C also is not correct. Instead of promising the matching funds, the State department representatives promised to investigate (or look into) the possibility of obtaining the matching funds.

Choice D is incorrect because the reading passage does not tell whether telephone surveys or mailed questionnaires provide more accurate information. Remember, the instructions for this question state that the question is to be answered based ONLY on the information in the applicable reading passage.

4. The correct answer is Choice C. Choice A and Choice C both begin with Sentence III, which certainly could be the logical first sentence of a paragraph. However, the next sentence (Sentence I) in Choice A leaves the initial topic of obtaining information from citizens. The third sentence in Choice A would be Sentence IV, *No community should formulate these goals without attempting to obtain the views of its citizenry.* The words *these goals* do not logically refer to anything in the previous two sentences, so Choice A is incorrect.

   Choice B also is incorrect because the word *also* in its first sentence (Sentence I) has nothing to logically refer to. *Also* would have to be used in a sentence that comes later in the paragraph.

   Choice D has the same problem as Choice A. Choice D begins with Sentence IV, which starts off, *No community should formulate these goals....* Again, the words *these goals* need to refer to something in a previous sentence about goals in order to be logically correct.

5. Choice B is correct. Here are the mathematical computations you might use to arrive at the correct answer of 81%:

   1. The reading passage states that the Smith Paint Company currently employs 2,000 persons. The first part of this question states that 75% of those current employees were hired during the first ten years that the company was in operation. By multiplying 75% by 2,000, you would find that 1,500 of the current employees were hired during the company's first ten years.

   2. The question asks about the first 13 years of the company's operation rather than just the first ten years. Therefore, you need the arithmetical information for the three years that immediately followed the first ten years. You know from the reading passage that the company has been operating for 20 years. You have the information for the first ten years. Twenty minus ten leaves the most recent ten years.

3. You know from the question that 40 persons were hired each year during the five-year period of time between the first ten years and the most recent five years. However, you need information about only the first three years. By multiplying 40 persons per year by three years, you would find that 120 people were hired during the first three years that came immediately after the first ten years of the company's operation.

4. Next, you would need to add 1,500 people (for the first ten years) and 120 people (for the next three years). That would give you a total of 1,620 people hired during the first 13 years.

5. The question asks for the percentage of the Smith Paint Company's total employees hired during its first 13 years. You know that the total number of employees is 2,000.The question then is: 1,620 people is what percentage of 2,000 people? By dividing 2,000 into 1,620, you would find that the correct answer is 81%.

Choice A is incorrect because it deals with only the first ten years that the company was in operation, rather than the first 13 years. If you took 1,500 people (from Step 1 in the explanatory material for the correct answer) and divided that number by 2,000 people, you would arrive at 75%, which is not correct.

Choice C is incorrect. If you correctly arrived at 1,500 people for the first ten years but then incorrectly dealt with the next five years instead of the next three years, you would end up with the wrong answer of 85%. First, you would multiply 40 people by five years and end up with 200 people. Next, you would add 200 to 1,500 and end up with 1,700 people. Finally, you would divide 1,700 by 2,000 and get 85%.

Choice D also is incorrect. If you correctly arrived at 1,500 people for the first ten years but then used the information for the most recent five years instead of the information for the five years that came just before the most recent five years, you would end up with the incorrect answer of 90%. First, you would find from the question that 15% of the total employees were hired in the past five years. Next, you would multiply 15% by 2,000 total employees and end up with 300. Next, you would add 1,500 employees and 300 employees, ending up with a total of 1,800 employees. By dividing 1,800 by 2,000, you would arrive at 90%.

6. Choice A is correct. Here are the mathematical computations you would need to make to arrive at the correct answer of $250,000:

    1. The reading passage states that the amount of Futuron proposed for manufacture each year is 1 million gallons. The question states that the possible profit per gallon would be $1.00. By multiplying $1.00 by 1,000,000, you would find that $1,000,000 would be the total possible profit to be made during the first year.

    2. The question states that the $1,000,000 possible profit would have to be reduced by 50% because of the purchase of new machinery, plus by an additional 25% due to the delay in establishing manufacturing facilities. The possible profit must, therefore, be reduced by 50% plus 25%, or by a total of 75%, leaving only 25% of the $1,000,000 as possible profit.

3. By multiplying 25% by $1,000,000, you would arrive at $250,000 as the actual profit which would be made.

Choice B is incorrect. If the two profit reductions were incorrectly multiplied by one another (50% times 25%) and the product (12 1/2%) added to 50%, there would have been a net reduction of 62 1/2%, yielding $375,000. However, the two profit reductions are independent of each other and should be added together.

Choice C also is incorrect. It would occur if you only took into account the 50% profit reduction. However, as the paragraph states, you must also deduct an additional 25% of the total profit.

Choice D ($750,000) would be made if you incorrectly multiplied the total profit reduction (75%) by $1,000,000. However, the question asks for the profit, not the profit reduction.

7. Both *indeterminate* and *inconclusive* mean *vague* and *indefinite,* so Choice D is correct. Choice A is incorrect, because the word *ineluctable* means inescapable or inevitable. The reading passage does not support the conclusion that the research results are incorrect or unreasonable, so Choice B and Choice C can be eliminated from consideration.

8. Choice D is correct. The reading passage states, *The sales were phenomenal, and there is a great demand for more Futuron to be manufactured. The profits to be made by increasing the manufacturing and sale of Futuron could place the Smith Paint Company in a leading role in the paint industry.* Since the sales of Futuron were phenomenal (remarkable; extraordinary), and there still is a great demand for it, the suggestion of considerable future profit is reasonable.

Choice A is not the most accurate conclusion based on the reading passage. The financial impact of decreasing the production of the traditional paint cannot be ascertained. Therefore, it is not certain that the proposed 50% reduction in the manufacturing of the Smith Paint Company's traditional paint would not financially injure that company. Certainly, Choice D is a more accurate conclusion.

Choice B is incorrect. A greater proportion of the employees being in favor of the proposed increase in Futuron production than not being in favor of it implies that over 50% of the employees are in favor of it. However, the reading passage states that most of the employees (which, logically, means over 50% of the employees) do not want the proposed change to occur.

Choice C also is not the most accurate conclusion. It states that the proposed increase in Futuron production would cause employees considerable health damage. The reading passage is not definite on this issue of health damage. It states, *Initial research indicates that negative physical reactions may result from working closely with the chemicals necessary....* How serious the health damage might be is not stated in the reading passage.

EXAMINATION SECTION
TEST 1

DIRECTIONS: Each question consists of several sentences which can be arranged in a logical sequence. For each question, select the choice which places the numbered sentences in the MOST logical sequence. *PRINT THE LETTER OF THE CORRECT ANSWER IN THE SPACE AT THE RIGHT.*

1. I. A body was found in the woods. 1.____
   II. A man proclaimed innocence.
   III. The owner of a gun was located.
   IV. A gun was traced.
   V. The owner of a gun was questioned.

   The CORRECT answer is:

   A. IV, III, V, II, I
   B. II, I, IV, III, V
   C. I, IV, III, V, II
   D. I, III, V, II, IV
   E. I, II, IV, III, V

2. I. A man was in a hunting accident. 2.____
   II. A man fell down a flight of steps.
   III. A man lost his vision in one eye.
   IV. A man broke his leg.
   V. A man had to walk with a cane.

   The CORRECT answer is:

   A. II, IV, V, I, III
   B. IV, V, I, III, II
   C. III, I, IV, V, II
   D. I, III, V, II, IV
   E. I, III, II, IV, V

3. I. A man is offered a new job. 3.____
   II. A woman is offered a new job.
   III. A man works as a waiter.
   IV. A woman works as a waitress.
   V. A woman gives notice.

   The CORRECT answer is:

   A. IV, II, V, III, I
   B. IV, II, V, I, III
   C. II, IV, V, III, I
   D. III, I, IV, II, V
   E. IV, III, II, V, I

4. I. A train left the station late. 4.____
   II. A man was late for work.
   III. A man lost his job.
   IV. Many people complained because the train was late.
   V. There was a traffic jam.

   The CORRECT answer is:

   A. V, II, I, IV, III
   B. V, I, IV, II, III
   C. V, I, II, IV, III
   D. I, V, IV, II, III
   E. II, I, IV, V, III

5. I. The burden of proof as to each issue is determined before trial and remains upon the same party throughout the trial. 5.____
II. The jury is at liberty to believe one witness' testimony as against a number of contradictory witnesses.
III. In a civil case, the party bearing the burden of proof is required to prove his contention by a fair preponderance of the evidence.
IV. However, it must be noted that a fair preponderance of evidence does not necessarily mean a greater number of witnesses.
V. The burden of proof is the burden which rests upon one of the parties to an action to persuade the trier of the facts, generally the jury, that a proposition he asserts is true.
VI. If the evidence is equally balanced, or if it leaves the jury in such doubt as to be unable to decide the controversy either way, judgment must be given against the party upon whom the burden of proof rests.

The CORRECT answer is:

A. III, II, V, IV, I, VI
B. I, II,VI,V,III,IV
C. III, IV, V, I, II, VI
D. V, I, III,VI, IV, II
E. I,V, III, VI, IV, II

6. I. If a parent is without assets and is unemployed, he cannot be convicted of the crime of non-support of a child. 6.____
II. The term *sufficient ability* has been held to mean sufficient financial ability.
III. It does not matter if his unemployment is by choice or unavoidable circumstances.
IV. If he fails to take any steps at all, he may be liable to prosecution for endangering the welfare of a child.
V. Under the penal law, a parent is responsible for the support of his minor child only if the parent is of *sufficient ability.*
VI. An indigent parent may meet his obligation by borrowing money or by seeking aid under the provisions of the Social Welfare Law.

The CORRECT answer is:

A. VI, I, V, III, II, IV
B. I, III, V, II, IV, VI
C. V, II, I, III, VI, IV
D. I, VI, IV, V, II, III
E. II, V, I, III, VI, IV

7. I. Consider, for example, the case of a rabble rouser who urges a group of twenty people to go out and break the windows of a nearby factory. 7.____
II. Therefore, the law fills the indicated gap with the crime of *inciting to riot.*
III. A person is considered guilty of inciting to riot when he urges ten or more persons to engage in tumultuous and violent conduct of a kind likely to create public alarm.
IV. However, if he has not obtained the cooperation of at least four people, he cannot be charged with unlawful assembly.
V. The charge of inciting to riot was added to the law to cover types of conduct which cannot be classified as either the crime of *riot* or the crime of *unlawful assembly.*
VI. If he acquires the acquiescence of at least four of them, he is guilty of unlawful assembly even if the project does not materialize.

The CORRECT answer is:

A. III, V, I, VI, IV, II
B. V, I, IV, VI, II, III
C. III, IV, I, V, II, VI
D. V, I, IV, VI, III, II
E. V, III, I, VI, IV, II

8. I. If, however, the rebuttal evidence presents an issue of credibility, it is for the jury to determine whether the presumption has, in fact, been destroyed. 8.____
II. Once sufficient evidence to the contrary is introduced, the presumption disappears from the trial.
III. The effect of a presumption is to place the burden upon the adversary to come forward with evidence to rebut the presumption.
IV. When a presumption is overcome and ceases to exist in the case, the fact or facts which gave rise to the presumption still remain.
V. Whether a presumption has been overcome is ordinarily a question for the court.
VI. Such information may furnish a basis for a logical inference.

The CORRECT answer is:

A. IV, VI, II, V, I, III
B. III, II, V, I, IV, VI
C. V, III, VI, IV, II, I
D. V, IV, I, II, VI, III
E. II, III, V, I, IV, VI

9. I. An executive may answer a letter by writing his reply on the face of the letter itself instead of having a return letter typed. 9.____
II. This procedure is efficient because it saves the executive's time, the typist's time, and saves office file space.
III. Copying machines are used in small offices as well as large offices to save time and money in making brief replies to business letters.
IV. A copy is made on a copying machine to go into the company files, while the original is mailed back to the sender.

The CORRECT answer is:

A. I, II, IV, III
B. I, IV, II, III
C. III, I, IV, II
D. III, IV, II, I

10. I. Most organizations favor one of the types but always include the others to a lesser degree. 10.____
II. However, we can detect a definite trend toward greater use of symbolic control.
III. We suggest that our local police agencies are today primarily utilizing material control.
IV. Control can be classified into three types: physical, material, and symbolic.

The CORRECT answer is:

A. IV, II, III, I
B. II, I, IV, III
C. III, IV, II, I
D. IV, I, III, II

11. I. Project residents had first claim to this use, followed by surrounding neighborhood children. 11.____
II. By contrast, recreation space within the project's interior was found to be used more often by both groups.
III. Studies of the use of project grounds in many cities showed grounds left open for public use were neglected and unused, both by residents and by members of the surrounding community.

IV. Project residents had clearly laid claim to the play spaces, setting up and enforcing unwritten rules for use.
V. Each group, by experience, found their activities easily disrupted by other groups, and their claim to the use of space for recreation difficult to enforce.

The CORRECT answer is:

A. IV, V, I, II, III
B. V, II, IV, III, I
C. I, IV, III, II, V
D. III, V, II, IV, I

12. I. They do not consider the problems correctable within the existing subsidy formula and social policy of accepting all eligible applicants regardless of social behavior and lifestyle. 12.____
II. A recent survey, however, indicated that tenants believe these problems correctable by local housing authorities and management within the existing financial formula.
III. Many of the problems and complaints concerning public housing management and design have created resentment between the tenant and the landlord.
IV. This same survey indicated that administrators and managers do not agree with the tenants.

The CORRECT answer is:

A. II, I, III, IV
B. I, III, IV, II
C. III, II, IV, I
D. IV, II, I, III

13. I. In single-family residences, there is usually enough distance between tenants to prevent occupants from annoying one another. 13.____
II. For example, a certain small percentage of tenant families has one or more members addicted to alcohol.
III. While managers believe in the right of individuals to live as they choose, the manager becomes concerned when the pattern of living jeopardizes others' rights.
IV. Still others turn night into day, staging lusty entertainments which carry on into the hours when most tenants are trying to sleep.
V. In apartment buildings, however, tenants live so closely together that any misbehavior can result in unpleasant living conditions.
VI. Other families engage in violent argument.

The CORRECT answer is:

A. III, II, V, IV, VI, I
B. I, V, II, VI, IV, III
C. II, V, IV, I, III, VI
D. IV, II, V, VI, III, I

14. I. Congress made the commitment explicit in the Housing Act of 1949, establishing as a national goal the realization of *a decent home and suitable environment for every American family.* 14.____
II. The result has been that the goal of decent home and suitable environment is still as far distant as ever for the disadvantaged urban family.
III. In spite of this action by Congress, federal housing programs have continued to be fragmented and grossly underfunded.
IV. The passage of the National Housing Act signalled a new federal commitment to provide housing for the nation's citizens.

The CORRECT answer is:

A. I, IV, III, II
B. IV, I, III, II
C. IV, I, II, III
D. II, IV, I, III

15. I. The greater expense does not necessarily involve *exploitation,* but it is often perceived as exploitative and unfair by those who are aware of the price differences involved, but unaware of operating costs. 15.____
II. Ghetto residents believe they are *exploited* by local merchants, and evidence substantiates some of these beliefs.
III. However, stores in low-income areas were more likely to be small independents, which could not achieve the economies available to supermarket chains and were, therefore, more likely to charge higher prices, and the customers were more likely to buy smaller-sized packages which are more expensive per unit of measure.
IV. A study conducted in one city showed that distinctly higher prices were charged for goods sold in ghetto stores than in other areas.

The CORRECT answer is:

A. IV, II, I, III
B. IV, I, III, II
C. II, IV, III, I
D. II, III, IV, I

KEY (CORRECT ANSWERS)

1. C
2. E
3. B
4. B
5. D
6. C
7. A
8. B
9. C
10. D
11. D
12. C
13. B
14. B
15. C

WRITTEN ENGLISH EXPRESSION

EXAMINATION SECTION
TEST 1

DIRECTIONS: In each of the sentences below, four portions are underlined and lettered. Read each sentence and decide whether any of the UNDERLINED parts contains an error in spelling, punctuation, or capitalization, or employs grammatical usage which would be inappropriate for carefully written English. If so, note the letter printed under the unacceptable form and indicate this choice in the space at the right. If all four of the underlined portions are acceptable as they stand, select the answer E.
(No sentence contains more than ONE unacceptable form.)

1. The revised procedure was quite different than the one which was employed up to that time. No error 1.____
procedure = A, quite = B, than = C, was = D, No error = E

2. Blinded by the storm that surrounded him, his plane kept going in circles. No error 2.____
Blinded = A, surrounded = B, kept going = C, circles. = D, No error = E

3. They should give the book to whoever they think deserves it . No error 3.____
should = A, whoever = B, they = C, it = D, No error = E

4. The government will not consent to your firm sending that package as second class matter. No error 4.____
government = A, firm = B, sending = C, second class = D, No error = E

5. She would have avoided all the trouble that followed if she would have waited ten minutes longer . No error 5.____
would have = A, that = B, would have = C, longer = D, No error = E

6. His poetry, when it was carefully examined, showed characteristics not unlike Wordsworth . No error 6.____
His = A, when = B, characteristics = C, Wordsworth = D, No error = E

7. In my opinion, (A) based upon long years of research, I think (B) the plan offered by my opponent is unsound, (C) because it is not founded (D) on true facts. No error (E) 7.____

8. The soldiers of Washington's (A) army at Valley Forge were (B) men ragged in appearance (C) but who were (D) noble in character. No error (E) 8.____

9. Rabbits have a distrust (A) of man due to (B) the fact that (C) they are so often (D) shot. No error (E) 9.____

10. This (A) is the man who (B) I believe is (C) best qualified (D) for the position. No error (E) 10.____

11. Her voice was not only (A) good, (B) but she (C) also very clearly enunciated. (D) No error (E) 11.____

12. Today he (A) is wearing a different (B) suit than (C) the one (D) he wore yesterday. No error (E) 12.____

13. Our work is (A) to improve the club; if anybody must (B) resign, let it not (C) be you or I (D). No error (E) 13.____

14. There was so much talking <u>in back of</u> (A) me <u>as</u> (B) I <u>could</u> (C) not <u>enjoy</u> (D) the music. <u>No error</u> (E) 14.____

15. <u>Being that</u> (A) he is that <u>kind of</u> (B) <u>boy</u> (C), he cannot be blamed <u>for</u> (D) the mistake. <u>No error</u> (E) 15.____

16. <u>The king, having read</u> (A) the speech, <u>he</u> (B) and the <u>queen</u> (C) <u>departed</u> (D). <u>No error</u> (E) 16.____

17. I <u>am</u> (A) <u>so tired</u> (B) I <u>can't</u> (C) <u>scarcely</u> (D) stand. <u>No error</u> (E) 17.____

18. We are <u>mailing bills</u> (A) to our customers <u>in Canada</u> (B), and, <u>being</u> (C) eager to clear our books before the new season opens, it is <u>to be hoped</u> (D) they will send their remittances promptly. <u>No error</u> (E) 18.____

19. <u>I</u> (A) <u>reluctantly</u> (B) <u>acquiesced</u> (C) to the <u>proposal</u> (D). <u>No error</u> (E) 19.____

20. <u>It</u> (A) <u>had lain</u> (B) <u>out</u> (C) in the rain <u>all night</u> (D). <u>No error</u> (E) 20.____

21. <u>If he would have</u> (A) <u>gone</u> (B) there, he <u>would have</u> (C) seen a <u>marvelous</u> (D) sight. <u>No error</u> (E) 21.____

22. The climate <u>of</u> (A) Asia Minor <u>is</u> (B) <u>somewhat</u> (C) like <u>Utah</u> (D). <u>No error</u> (E) 22.____

23. If everybody (A) did (B) unto others (C) as they would wish (D) others to do unto them, this world would be a paradise. No error (E) 23.____

24. This (A) was the jockey whom (B) I saw was (C) most likely to win (D) the race. No error (E) 24.____

25. The only (A) food the general demanded (B) was (C) potatoes (D). No error (E) 25.____

KEY (CORRECT ANSWERS)

1. C
2. A
3. B
4. B
5. C
6. D
7. B
8. D
9. B
10. E
11. C
12. C
13. D
14. B
15. A
16. A
17. C
18. C
19. E
20. E
21. A
22. D
23. D
24. B
25. E

TEST 2

DIRECTIONS: In each of the sentences below, four portions are underlined and lettered. Read each sentence and decide whether any of the UNDERLINED parts contains an error in spelling, punctuation, or capitalization, or employs grammatical usage which would be inappropriate for carefully written English. If so, note the letter printed under the unacceptable form and indicate this choice in the space at the right. If all four of the underlined portions are acceptable as they stand, select the answer E. (No sentence contains more than ONE unacceptable form.)

1. A party like (A) that (B) only (C) comes (D) once a year. No error (E) — 1.____

2. Our's (A) is (B) a (C) swift moving (D) age. No error (E) — 2.____

3. The healthy (A) climate soon restored (B) him to (C) his accustomed (D) vigor. No error (E) — 3.____

4. They (A) needed six typists and hoped that only (B) that many (C) would (D) apply for the position. No error (E) — 4.____

5. He interviewed (A) people whom (B) he thought had something (C) to impart. (D) No error (E) — 5.____

6. Neither (A) of his three sisters is (B) older than (C) he. (D) No error (E) — 6.____

7. Since (A) he is that (B) kind (C) of a (D) boy, he cannot be expected to cooperate with us. No error (E) — 7.____

8. ____

8.	When passing	through	the tunnel, the air pressure	affected	our	ears.	No error
	A	B		C	D		E

9. ____

9.	The story having	a sad ending,	it	never	achieved	popularity	among	the students.	No error
	A		B		C		D		E

10. ____

10.	Since	we are both hungry,	shall	we go	somewhere	for lunch	?	No error
	A		B		C		D	E

11. ____

11.	Will	you please	bring	this book	down to	the library and give it to my friend	,	who is waiting for it?	No error
	A		B		C		D		E

12. ____

12.	You	may	have	the book; I	am	finished	with	it.	No error
		A	B		C		D		E

13. ____

13.	I	don't	know	if	I	should	mention	it	to her or not.	No error
		A		B		C		D		E

14. ____

14.	Philosophy is not	a subject	which	has to do	with philosophers and mathematics	only.	No error
		A	B	C		D	E

15. ____

15.	The thoughts of the scholar	in his library	are little different	than	the old woman who first said,	"It's	no use crying over spilt milk	."	No error
		A		B		C		D	E

16. ____

16.	A complete	system	of philosophical ideas	are	implied	in many simple	utterances.	No error
		A		B	C		D	E

17. Even <u>if</u> (A) one has never put <u>them</u> (B) into words, <u>his</u> (C) ideas <u>compose</u> (D) a kind of a philosophy. <u>No error</u> (E) 17.____

18. Perhaps it <u>is</u> (A) <u>well enough</u> (B) that most <u>people</u> (C) do not attempt this <u>formulation.</u> (D) <u>No error</u> (E) 18.____

19. <u>Leading their</u> (A) ordered lives, this <u>confused</u> (B) <u>body</u> (C) of ideas and feelings <u>is</u> (D) sufficient. <u>No error</u> (E) 19.____

20. Why <u>should</u> (A) we <u>insist upon</u> (B) <u>them</u> (C) <u>formulating</u> (D) it? <u>No error</u> (E) 20.____

21. <u>Since</u> (A) it includes <u>something</u> (B) of the wisdom of the ages, it is <u>adequate</u> (C) for the <u>purposes</u> (D) of ordinary life. <u>No error</u> (E) 21.____

22. Therefore, I <u>have sought</u> (A) to make a pattern <u>of mine,</u> (B) <u>and so</u> (C) there were, early moments of <u>my trying</u> (D) to find out what were the elements with which I had to deal; <u>No error</u> (E) 22.____

23. I <u>wanted</u> (A) <u>to get</u> (B) <u>what</u> (C) knowledge I <u>could</u> (D) about the general structure of the universe. <u>No error</u> (E) 23.____

24. I wanted to <u>know</u> (A) <u>if</u> (B) life <u>per se</u> (C) had any meaning or <u>whether</u> (D) I must strive to give it one. <u>No error</u> (E) 24.____

25. <u>So,</u> (A) in a <u>desultory</u> (B) way, I <u>began</u> (C) <u>to read.</u> (D) <u>No error</u> (E) 25.____

KEY (CORRECT ANSWERS)

1.	C	11.	B
2.	A	12.	C
3.	A	13.	B
4.	C	14.	D
5.	B	15.	B
6.	A	16.	B
7.	D	17.	A
8.	A	18.	C
9.	A	19.	A
10.	E	20.	C

21. E
22. C
23. C
24. B
25. E

WRITTEN ENGLISH EXPRESSION
EXAMINATION SECTION
TEST 1

DIRECTIONS: The following questions are designed to test your knowledge of grammar, sentence structure, correct usage, and punctuation. In each group there is one sentence that contains no errors. Select the letter of the CORRECT sentence. *PRINT THE LETTER OF THE CORRECT ANSWER IN THE SPACE AT THE RIGHT.*

1. A. A low ceiling is when the atmospheric conditions make flying inadvisable. 1.____
   B. They couldn't tell who the card was from.
   C. No one but you and I are to help him.
   D. What kind of a teacher would you like to be?
   E. To him fall the duties of foster parent.

2. A. They couldn't tell whom the cable was from. 2.____
   B. We like these better than those kind.
   C. It is a test of you more than I.
   D. The person in charge being him, there can be no change in policy.
   E. Chicago is larger than any city in Illinois.

3. A. Do as we do for the celebration. 3.____
   B. Do either of you care to join us?
   C. A child's food requirements differ from the adult.
   D. A large family including two uncles and four grandparents live at the hotel.
   E. Due to bad weather, the game was postponed.

4. A. If they would have done that they might have succeeded. 4.____
   B. Neither the hot days or the humid nights annoy our Southern visitor.
   C. Some people do not gain favor because they are kind of tactless.
   D. No sooner had the turning point come than a new issue arose.
   E. I wish that I was in Florida now.

5. A. We haven't hardly enough tine. 5.____
   B. Immigration is when people come into a foreign country to live.
   C. After each side gave their version, the affair was over with.
   D. Every one of the cars were tagged by the police.
   E. He either will fail in his attempt or will seek other employment.

6. A. They can't seem to see it when I explain the theory. 6.____
   B. It is difficult to find the genuine signature between all those submitted.
   C. She can't understand why they don't remember who to give the letter to
   D. Every man and woman in America is interested in his tax bill.
   E. Honor as well as profit are to be gained by these studies.

7. A. He arrived safe. 7.____
B. I do not have any faith in John running for office.
C. The musicians began to play tunefully and keeping the proper tempo indicated for the selection.
D. Mary's maid of honor bought the kind of an outfit suitable for an afternoon wedding.
E. If you would have studied the problem carefully you would have found the solution more quickly.

8. A. The new plant is to be electric lighted. 8.____
B. The reason the speaker was offended was that the audience was inattentive.
C. There appears to be conditions that govern his behavior.
D. Either of the men are influential enough to control the situation.
E. The gallery with all its pictures were destroyed.

9. A. If you would have listened more carefully, you would have heard your name called. 9.____
B. Did you inquire if your brother were returning soon?
C. We are likely to have rain before nightfall.
D. Let's you and I plan next summer's vacation together.
E. The man whom I thought was my friend deceived me.

10. A. There's a man and his wife waiting for the doctor since early this morning. 10.____
B. The owner of the market with his assistants is applying the most modern principles of merchandise display.
C. Every one of the players on both of the competing teams were awarded a gold watch.
D. The records of the trial indicated that, even before attaining manhood, the murderer's parents were both dead.
E. We had no sooner entered the room when the bell rang.

11. A. Why don't you start the play like I told you? 11.____
B. I didn't find the construction of the second house much different from that of the first one I saw.
C. "When", inquired the child, "Will we begin celebrating my birthday?"
D. There isn't nothing left to do but not to see him anymore.
E. There goes the last piece of cake and the last spoonful of ice cream.

12. A. The child could find neither the shoe or the stocking. 12.____
B. The musicians began to play tunefully and keeping the proper tempo indicated for the selection.
C. The amount of curious people who turned out for Opening Night was beyond calculation.
D. I fully expected that the children would be at their desks and to find them ready to begin work,
E. "Indeed," mused the poll-taker, "the winning candidate is much happier than I."

13. A. Just as you said, I find myself gaining weight. 13.____
B. A teacher should leave the capable pupils engage in creative activities.
C. The teacher spoke continually during the entire lesson, which, of course, was poor procedure.
D. We saw him steal into the room, pick up the letter, and tear it's contents to shreds.
E. It is so dark that I can't hardly see.

14. A. The new schedule of working hours and rates was satis factory to both employees and employer. 14.____
B. Many common people feel keenly about the injustices of Power Politics.
C. Mr. and Mrs. Burns felt that their grandchild was awfully cute when he waved good-bye.
D. The tallest of the twins was also the most intelligent,
E. Please come here and try and help me finish this piece of work.

15. A. My younger brother insists that he is as tall as me. 15.____
B. Suffering from a severe headache all day, one dose of the prescribed medicine relieved me,
C. "Please let my brothers and I help you with your packages," said Frank to Mrs. Powers.
D. Every one of the rooms we visited had displays of pupils' work in them.
E. Do you intend bringing most of the refreshments yourself?

16. A. The telephone linesmen, working steadily at their task during the severe storm, the telephones soon began to ring again. 16.____
B. Meat, as well as fruits and vegetables, is considered essential to a proper diet.
C. He looked like a real good boxer that night in the ring.
D. The man has worked steadily for fifteen years before he decided to open his own business.
E. The winters were hard and dreary, nothing could live without shelter.

17. A. No one can foretell when I will have another opportunity like that one again. 17.____
B. The last group of paintings shown appear really to have captured the most modern techniques,
C. We searched high and low, both in the attic and cellar, but were unsuccessful in locating mementos.
D. None of the guests was able to give the rules of the game accurately.
E. When you go to the library tomorrow, please bring this book to the librarian in the reference room.

18. A. After the debate, every one of the speakers realized that, given another chance, he could have done better. 18.____
B. The reason given by the physician for the patient's trouble was because of his poor eating habits.
C. The fog was so thick that the driver couldn't hardly see more than ten feet ahead.
D. I suggest that you present the medal to who you think best.
E. I don't approve of him going along.

19. A. A decision made by a man without much deliberation is sometimes no different than a slow one. 19.____
B. By the time Mr. Brown's son will graduate Dental School, he will be twenty-six years of age.
C. Who did you predict would win the election?
D. The auctioneer had less stamps to sell this year than last year.
E. Being that he is occupied, I shall not disturb him.

20. A. Having pranced into the arena with little grace and unsteady hoof for the jumps ahead, the driver reined his horse. 20.____
B. Once the dog wagged it's tail, you knew it was a friendly animal.
C. Like a great many artists, his life was a tragedy.
D. When asked to choose corn, cabbage, or potatoes, the diner selected the latter.
E. The record of the winning team was among the most noteworthy of the season.

21. A. The maid wasn't so small that she couldn't reach the top window for cleaning. 21.____
B. Many people feel that powdered coffee produces a really good flavor.
C. Would you mind me trying that coat on for size?
D. This chair looks much different than the chair we selected in the store.
E. I wish that he would have talked to me about the lesson before he presented it.

22. A. After trying unsuccessfully to land a job in the city, Will located in the country on a farm. 22.____
B. On the last attempt, the pole-vaulter came nearly to getting hurt.
C. The observance of Armistice Day throughout the world offers an opportunity to reflect on the horrors of war.
D. Outside of the mistakes in spelling, the child's letter was a very good one.
E. The annual income of New York is far greater than Florida.

23. A. Scissors is always dangerous for a child to handle. 23.____
B. I assure you that I will not yield to pressure to sell my interest.
C. Ask him if he has recall of the incident which took place at our first meeting.
D. The manager felt like as not to order his usher-captain to surrender his uniform,
E. Everyone on the boat said their prayers when the storm grew worse.

24. A. The mother of the bride climaxed the occasion by exclaiming, "I want my children should be happy forever." 24.____
B. We read in the papers where the prospects for peace are improving.
C. "Can I share the cab with you?" was frequently heard during the period of gas rationing.
D. The man was enamored with his friend"s sister.
E. Had the police suspected the ruse, they would have taken proper precautions.

25. A. The teacher admonished the other students neither to speak to John, nor should they annoy him. 25.____
B. Fortunately we had been told that there was but one service station in that area.
C. An usher seldom rises above a theatre manager.
D. The epic, "Gone With the Wind," is supposed to have taken place during the Civil War Era.
E. Now that she has been graduated she should be encouraged to make her own choice as to the career she is to follow.

KEY (CORRECT ANSWERS)

1. E
2. A
3. A
4. D
5. E
6. D
7. A
8. B
9. C
10. B
11. B
12. E
13. A
14. A
15. E
16. B
17. D
18. A
19. C
20. E
21. B
22. C
23. B
24. E
25. B

TEST 2

DIRECTIONS: The following questions are designed to test your knowledge of grammar, sentence structure, correct usage, and punctuation. In each group, there is one sentence that contains no errors. Select the letter of the CORRECT sentence. *PRINT THE LETTER OF THE CORRECT ANSWER IN THE SPACE AT THE RIGHT.*

1. A. Shall you be at home, let us say, on Sunday at two o'clock? 1.____
   B. We see Mr. Lewis take his car out of the garage daily, newly polished always.
   C. We have no place to keep our rubbers, only in the hall closet.
   D. Isn't it true what you told me about the best way to prepare for an examination?
   E. Mathematics is among my favorite subjects.

2. A. The host thought the guests were of the hungry kinds so he prepared much food. 2.____
   B. The museum is often visited by students who are fond of early inventions, and especially patent attorneys.
   C. I rose to nominate the man who most of us felt was the most diligent worker in the group.
   D. The child was sent to the store to purchase a bottle of milk, and brought home fresh rolls, too.
   E. Hidden away in the closet, I found the long-lost purse.

3. A. The garden tool was sent to be sharpened, and a new handle to be put on. 3.____
   B. At the end of her vacation, Joan came home with little money, but which systematic thrift soon overcame.
   C. We people have opportunities to show the rest of the world how real democracy functions.
   D. The guide paddled along, then fell in a reverie which he related the history of the region.
   E. No sooner had the curtain dropped when the audience shouted its approval in chorus.

4. A. The data you need is to be made available shortly. 4.____
   B. The first few strokes of the brush were enough to convince me that Tom could paint much better than me.
   C. We inquired if we could see the owner of the store, after we waited for one hour.
   D. The highly-strung parent was aggravated by the slightest noise that the baby made.
   E. We should have investigated the cause of the noise by bringing the car to a halt.

5. A. The police, investigating the crime, were successful in discovering only one possibly valuable clue. 5.____
   B. Due to an unexpected change in plans, the violin soloist did not perform.
   C. Besides being awarded a Bachelor's degree at college, the scientist has since received many honorary degrees.
   D. The data offered in advance of the recent Presidential election seems to have possessed elements of inaccuracy.
   E. I don't believe your the only one who has been asked to come here.

6. A. I don't quite see that I will be able to completely finish the job in time. 6.____
B. By my statement, I infer that you are guilty of the offense as charged.
C. Wasn't it strange that they wouldn't let no one see the body?
D. I hope that this is the kind of rolls you requested me to buy.
E. The storekeeper distributed cigars as bonuses between his many customers.

7. A. He said he preferred the climate of Florida to California. 7.____
B. Because of the excessive heat, a great amount of fruit juice was drunk by the guests.
C. This week's dramatic presentation was neither as lively nor as entertaining as last week.
D. The fashion expert believed that no one could develop new creations more successfully than him.
E. A collection of Dicken's works is a "must" for every library.

8. A. There was such a large amount of books on the floor that I couldn't find a place for my rocking chair. 8.____
B. Walking up the rickety stairs, the bottle slipped from his hands and smashed.
C. The reason they granted his request was because he had a good record.
D. Little Tommy was proud that the teacher always asked him to bring messages to the office.
E. That kind of orange is grown only in Florida.

9. A. The new mayor is a resident of this city for thirty years. 9.____
B. Do you mean to imply that had he not missed that shot he would have won?
C. Next term I shall be studying French and history.
D. I read in last night's paper where the sales tax is going to be abolished.
E. In order to prevent breakage, she placed a sheet of paper between each of the plates when she packed them.

10. A. To have children vie against one another is psychologically unsound. 10.____
B. Would anyone else care to discuss his baby?
C. He was interested and aware of the problem.
D. I sure would like to discover if he is motivating the lesson properly.
E. The cloth was first lain on a flat surface; then it was pressed with a hot iron.

11. A. She graduated Barnard College twenty-five years ago. 11.____
B. He studied the violin since he was seven.
C. She is not so diligent a researcher as her classmate.
D. He discovered that the new data corresponds with the facts disclosed by Werner.
E. How could he enjoy the television program; the dog was barking and the baby was crying.

12. A. You have three alternatives: law, dentistry, or teaching. 12.____
B. If I would have worked harder, I would have accomplished my purpose.
C. He affected a rapid change of pace and his opponents were outdistanced.
D. He looked prosperous, although he had been unemployed for a year.
E. The engine not only furnishes power but light and heat as well.

13. A. The children shared one anothers toys and seemed quite happy. 13.____
B. They lay in the sun for many hours, getting tanned.
C. The reproduction arrived, and had been hung in the living room.
D. First begin by calling the roll.
E. Tell me where you hid it; no one shall ever find it.

14. A. Deliver these things to whomever arrives first. 14.____
B. Everybody but she and me is going to the conference.
C. If the number of patrons is small, we can serve them.
D. When each of the contestants find their book, the debate may begin.
E. Some people, farmers in particular, lament the substitution of butter by margarine.

15. A. After his illness, he stood in the country three weeks. 15.____
B. If you wish to effect a change, submit your suggestions.
C. It is silly to leave children play with knives.
D. Play a trick on her by spilling water down her neck.
E. There was such a crowd of people at the crossing we couldn't hardly get on the bus.

16. A. This is a time when all of us must show our faith and devotion to our country. 16.____
B. Either you or I are certain to be elected president of the new club.
C. The interpellation of the Minister of Finance forced him to explain his policies.
D. After hoisting the anchor and removing the binnacle, the ship was ready to set sail.
E. Please bring me a drink of cold water from the refrigerator.

17. A. Mistakes in English, when due to carelessness or haste, can easily be rectified. 17.____
B. Mr. Jones is one of those persons who will try to keep a promise and usually does.
C. Being very disturbed by what he had heard, Fred decided to postpone his decision.
D. There is a telephone at the other end of the corridor which is constantly in use.
E. In his teaching, he always kept the childrens' interests and needs in mind.

18. A. The lazy pupil, of course, will tend to write the minimum amount of words acceptable. 18.____
B. His success as a political leader consisted mainly of his ability to utter platitudes in a firm and convincing manner.
C. To be cognizant of current affairs, a person must not only read newspapers and magazines but also recent books by recognized authorities.
D. Although we intended to have gone fishing, the sudden outbreak of a storm caused us to change our plans.
E. It is the colleges that must take the responsibility for encouraging greater flexibility in the high-school curriculum.

19. A. "I am sorry," he said, "but John's answer was 'No'." 19.____
B. A spirited argument followed between those who favored and opposed Marie's expulsion from the club.
C. Whether a forward child should be humored or punished often depends upon the circumstances.
D. Excessive alcoholism is certainly not conducive with efficient performance of one's work.
E. Stroking his beard thoughtfully, an idea suddenly came to him.

20. A. "Take care, my children," he said sadly, "lest you not be deceived." 20.____
B. Those continuous telephone calls are preventing Betty from completing her homework.
C. They dug deep into the earth at the spot indicated on the map, but they found nothing.
D. We petted and cozened the little girl until she finally stopped weeping.
E. There was, in the mail, an inquiry for a house by a young couple with two or three bedrooms.

21. A. Please fill in the required information on the application form and return same by April 15. 21.____
B. Tom was sitting there idly, watching the clouds scud across the sky.
C. We started for home so that our parents would not suspect that anything out of the ordinary took place.
D. The sudden abatement from the storm enabled the ladies to resume their journey.
E. Each of the twelve members were agreed that the accused man was innocent.

22. A. The number of gifted students not continuing their education beyond secondary school present a nationwide problem. 22.____
B. A man's animadversions against those he considers his enemies are usually reflections of his own inadequacies.
C. The alembic of his fevered imagination produced some of the greatest romantic poetry of his era.
D. The first case of smallpox dates back more than 3000 years and has gone unchecked until recently.
E. He promised to go irregardless of the rain or snow.

23. A. The child picked up several of the coracles, which he had seen glittering in the sand, and brought them to his mother. 23.____
B. He muttered in dejected tones – and no one contradicted him – "We have failed."
C. A girl whom I believed to be she waved cheerily to me from a passing automobile.
D. We discovered that she was a former resident of our own neighborhood who eloped some years ago with a milkman.
E. It looks now like he will not be promoted after all.

24. A. Mary is the kind of a person on whom you can depend in any emergency. 24.____
B. I am sure that either applicant can fill the job you offer competently and efficiently.
C. Although we searched the entire room, the scissors was not to be found.
D. Being that you are here, we can proceed with the discussion.
E. In spite of our warning whistle, the huge ship continued to sail athwart our course.

25. A. The salaries earned by college graduates vary as much if not more than those earned by high school graduates. 25.____
B. The apothegms that he felt to be so witty were all too often either trite or platitudinous.
C. She read the letter carefully, took out one of the pages, and tore it into small pieces.
D. A young man, who hopes to succeed, must be diligent in his work and alert to his opportunities.
E. No one should plan a long journey for pleasure in these days.

KEY (CORRECT ANSWERS)

1. A
2. C
3. C
4. E
5. A
6. D
7. B
8. E
9. B
10. B
11. C
12. D
13. E
14. C
15. B
16. C
17. A
18. E
19. C
20. C
21. B
22. C
23. B
24. E
25. B